CW00763616

Magna Carta

A Captivating Guide to the History of the Great Charter and its Influence on Medieval England and the Rest of the World

Contents

Introduction

The Magna Carta is celebrated as one of the most important documents in human history. It is the main source of constitutional law around the world, promising people liberties and protection from the arbitrary power of the government. However, it is also a set of promises extorted in bad faith from an unwilling king, and these promises dealt with the problems of the 13th-century aristocracy. Among the ordinary problems of fees, customs, and land law, greater ideas found their way into the document, revolutionary ideas that would change the world. However, in 1215, they were sparse, mentioned here and there in the form of high ideals more than in the form of a law.

Some parts of the Magna Carta are still quoted, such as clauses that deal with justice before peers, freedom from unlawful imprisonment, freedom of the church, and so on. However, in medieval times, these clauses did not have the same meaning as they do today. The Magna Carta showed itself to be a flexible document with ideas that could be bent and transformed to suit the needs of the new times.

The role of the Magna Carta in 1215 wasn't so much to grant freedoms to the citizens of the English Kingdom. It was a tool that would pin down a king and stop him from using excessive power to tax his own people or take away baronial possessions at his royal whim. When observed in the light of the medieval times from which it sprouted, the Magna Carta ought to be dead, remembered only by history and scholars. Instead, it is very much alive today, and it is even celebrated as the most hallowed document ever to be written. Numerous countries have based their constitutional laws upon the Magna Carta and admire it as the foundation of Western liberties, democracy, and the rule of law.

For all those who wonder, this book offers the answers to how events leading up to and following the penning of this important document unfolded. Starting with the background story of the unjust rule of King John, this book tells of the birth of the Magna Carta, its failure, its resurrection, and its transformation into the laws of today.

Chapter 1 – King John

John was the youngest son of Henry II, King of England. As such, he was named "Lackland" because he couldn't possibly inherit any lands that were under the rule of his father. However, he was the favorite son, and Henry even considered naming him his successor. This would cause unrest within the kingdom, and the throne was passed to John's older brother, King Richard. John tried, unsuccessfully, to raise a rebellion against the rule of his brother while Richard was fighting in the Third Crusade. Upon his return to England, Richard made peace with John and even named him his successor. As Richard had no children, John inherited the throne and was crowned king in 1199. He became the ruler of England, Normandy, Anjou, Maine, Touraine, and Aquitaine— territories that historians often refer to as the Angevin Empire even though, officially, it was a kingdom. The territories ruled by the Angevins made up the largest landmass in Europe governed by a single ruler.

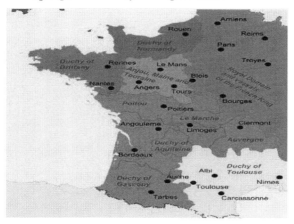

The Angevin continental empire in orange

(Source:
https://en.wikipedia.org/wiki/John,_King_of_England#/media/File:Angevin_empire.svg)

During his first five years of rule, John lost the continental part of the Angevin Empire. His unwillingness to fight, and the fact that he often ran away from battle, earned him a new nickname: among his troops, he was known as John the "Softsword." His main enemy was

Philip II, King of France, whose life goal was the destruction of Angevin rule in the French territories. Philip II was an excellent politician, a ruthless ruler, and he had a great appetite for power. He expanded the territories of the Kingdom of France, taking back provinces previously conquered by English kings. He even conquered the Duchy of Normandy, ancestral territory of the Angevin kings, striking a tremendous blow to King John.

John managed to quickly recover from all the losses in France. In 1206, England and France established a truce, and John turned his attention to governing England. The war with France was a disaster for the economy, and the king needed money. John raised taxes on everyone. Even the church was forced to contribute. Nobles, townsmen, and Jews were all pressed into paying unreasonable taxes. John was so successful in collecting the wealth that, by 1212, he had accumulated over £130,000 (about $200 million) in coins, which he hid in various castles that acted as royal treasuries.

A great deal of the gathered treasure caused John's conflict with the church because he was confiscating church lands and selling them to the nobles. This conflict arose when the Archbishop of Canterbury, Thomas Becket, died. The king used his authority to proclaim his own man, a bishop of Norwich's successor, to the position. Pope Innocent III had a different idea. He did not like John's idea of the king's authority over the church. John wasn't the only ruler of England to claim authority over the church; in fact, they all did. Even the most pious and religious William the Conqueror believed in state power over religion. This everlasting conflict would eventually lead to the separation of the English church during the rule of Henry VIII in the 16th century.

Pope Innocent III was determined to appoint a friend from his young student days, Stephen Langton, as the new Archbishop of Canterbury. King John opposed Langton for several reasons. He wanted his own man in the crucial religious position, and he did not trust Langton because he was schooled in Paris. Also, his brother was employed by Philip II of France for the same position in the French Notre Dame. John saw Langton as a politically inappropriate person for the position of archbishop in England. However, Pope Innocent convinced the delegation of the Christ Church in Canterbury to elect

Langton as the new archbishop even though John objected with passion. In retaliation, he started confiscating church properties, thus escalating the conflict between the church and the state. To punish England for the confiscated lands, Pope Innocent imposed severe ecclesiastical penalties throughout the country. In 1208, he laid an interdict on England that prevented its church officials from performing certain religious rights and services. In 1209, he personally excommunicated John, seeing that the king wouldn't back down and give up the cause. John decided his financial gains from this conflict would, by far, surpass the risks he was taking with his immortal soul. In fact, the financial gain from the interdict is estimated to be around £60,000 (about $100 million), which was equal to two years' gross annual revenue.

With a rich royal treasury and a firm grip on his rule in England, John started concentrating on expanding his kingdom. However, this time he did not look toward France because he knew he had no chance to regain the lost territories there. Instead, he concentrated on the Celtic lands—Ireland, Wales, and Scotland. He disciplined the Anglo-Irish barons and reinforced his rule in their lands, thus conquering north Wales. In addition, he invaded Scotland, where he gained control over succession rights.

During King John's Welsh expedition, a plot against his life and his rule was brewing. The barons of England were planning to assassinate him and replace him with Simon de Montfort, the leader of the Albigensian Crusade, a war against the Cathars in southern France. John learned about this plot on August 16th, two days after the mass hanging of Welsh hostages, which had the purpose of shocking the rebellious citizens of Wales. Afraid for his life, the king abandoned the Welsh expedition and demanded hostages from rebelling barons be sent to the court. John suspected everyone and wouldn't leave his chambers without an armed escort. He bullied his opponents to the extent that two of the important barons, Robert Fitzwalter and Eustace de Vesci, fled to France and joined the forces of King Philip II. However, soon after the initial shock, John reversed his policies and started treating his opponents with more respect. In truth, the king hoped to convince some of the barons to support him. Instead, his strength as a ruler collapsed, and he was thereafter seen as a weak, desperate king whose failures and despotic rule angered the barons.

The English barons were the ones who benefitted the most from the conquest of the French territories by the previous kings. Consequently, their loss was tremendous when John lost all the continental territories. Their castles and lands were now owned by the French king, who had the right to give them to his own nobles. This meant that the English barons lost their source of income, a fact about which they could not be indifferent. It wasn't just the income the barons were worried about, however. Just as kings, they were ambitious men who sought to transfer their titles and territories to their heirs and marry their sons and daughters into well-established dynasties that would bring them riches and political security. Losing the French territories, the barons were unable to pay their debt to King John, and their English lands were seized. The first to be forfeited for non-payment of debt in 1207 was the Earldom of Leicester. In the following year, the lands of John's favorite, William de Braose (or de Briouze), followed. William was exiled, and his wife and son became John's prisoners. It is generally believed the two of them were starved to death while locked away in Windsor Castle. John interpreted the existing laws, and he took the liberty to come up with new ones as he saw fit. He tried to excuse himself by explaining that he was merely punishing those who did not pay their debts to the Crown. However, the barons had their own interpretation of the laws, and they saw John's rule as atrocious. To them, it seemed the king had too much power and had to be stopped.

In France, Fitzwalter and Vesci found sympathy with King Philip II and the papal legates. They complained about John's rule and attacked him personally, telling stories of John's infidelity, in which he took married women—mostly of noble origins—as his mistresses. It is not clear whether these stories were true or simply the fabrications of barons who sought support from the French court, yet John is remembered for his infidelity. The barons told the papal legate Pandulf Verraccio of their decision to rebel against the English king due to the interdict he brought upon his own country. They also said they could not serve a king who was excommunicated. Fitzwalter and Vesci gained allies in addition to King Philip and the Vatican legates. They also gained support from exiled Englishmen who sought refuge in France, such as Giles de Braose (son of William de Braose), the Bishop of Hereford, and Stephen Langton.

John had two separate oppositions to his rule: the barons and the Vatican. Until the events in Paris, these two sides of the opposition were distant from each other. With Philip II acting as a mediator, however, the barons and the Vatican began to work together and were unified against a common enemy, the King of England. John was aware of this unification, and he tried to break them apart by making a deal with the pope. On May 15, 1213, at Ewell near Dover, the king formally surrendered the kingdom of England to the papal legate Pandulf. At the same time, he planned a new invasion of France, with which he tried to satisfy his supporters and gain new allies in alienated barons. However, the French, with their Flemish allies, defeated John's army on July 24, 1214, at the battle of Bouvines. Consequently, John promised Pope Innocent III that he would restore the lands of his main baronial opponents, Fitzwalter and Vesci. King John was defeated not only in battle but also in diplomacy. The worst blow he took was the exhaustion of his royal treasuries. Without money, he could not defend himself against his political enemies. He was naked in front of the opposition, and they had no reason to spare him.

Chapter 2 – The Path to Runnymede

In October 1214, John was back in England from his failed French expedition, where he was immediately faced with the revolt of the taxpayers. The empty royal treasure demanded higher taxes once again, which the citizens could not bear. Accordingly, the opposition at home started taking its shape and structure. The moment was perfect since the leaders of the opposition, Fitzwalter, and Vesci, were back. As they were the first to be suspected of revolt, the two nobles were forced to change their strategy.

Typically, a revolt against a king had in mind a suitable replacement that would occupy the throne. In John's case, there was no suitable replacement. He made sure to get rid of every potential successor to the crown, and his own children were simply too young to pose a threat. Fitzwalter, Vesci, and other barons could not allow themselves to be rebels without a cause. The solution was to rebel not against the king but against his idea of how he should rule. They devised a set of legal and governmental reforms that would restrict the king's power and grant themselves a set of new liberties. These reforms were embodied in the form of a charter, which later the king would recognize as the Great Charter of the Liberties.

A new name rose in the English political scene of the 13th century— Stephen Langton. Langton was appointed the Archbishop of Canterbury in 1207. After his delayed appointment as archbishop, Langton swore fealty to King John, who at first opposed his installment in Canterbury. The pope instructed Langton to do everything in his power to bring peace to the king and to the kingdom. This meant he would be expected to behave as a mediator between two opposing sides, the king and the revolting barons. In 1213, the archbishop lifted the king's excommunication, and John, in return, swore to protect the kingdom and the church. He also swore to maintain the favorable laws and get rid of the unjust ones, as well as to provide justice for everyone equally. However, the barons were free to interpret the oath of their king as they wished, and they claimed it meant the restoration of ancient baronial liberties. They invoked the Coronation Charter of Henry I, which would allow the barons to enjoy the rights that John had managed to take from them. This charter was meant to bind the king to treating nobles, church officials, and individuals in accordance with the law. The over-taxation of the barons was condemned by the charter, as well as any form of corruption. However, the Coronation Charter of Henry I was ignored by the king until 1213. Rumor has it that Langton himself reminded the barons of this charter and their guaranteed rights; however, even the contemporary chronicler Roger of Wendover admits that this was just a rumor, and there is no concrete evidence for Langton's involvement.

Even though King John issued his own charter on the day of his coronation, promising that his duty was to provide and secure liberty and safety for all the people of England, the barons did not trust him. For this reason, they chose to invoke Henry's Coronation Charter. Furthermore, the older charter was more promising than John's. It detailed topics such as inheritance, marriage, wardship, and more—all points over which the barons had argued with the king. John's charter was eloquent and used vague words, but the barons wanted practical solutions to the problems they were facing, not distant promises of a better future. The barons were aware that Henry's charter needed reworking to appeal to their troubles and their times, but it served as a good foundation for the reconstruction of the law and government.

On January 6, 1215, King John traveled to London to meet with the rebellious barons. The day was symbolic, as it was the last day of Christmas when, in old English tradition, kingship was celebrated. John wore the crown and expected his subjects to respect the symbolism of the day. However, the barons came armed and prepared, allowing no chance for the king to sway them from their determined path. Already politically weak, John lost the initiative. The meeting took place in the new Temple in London, an English seat of power belonging to the order of the Knights Templar. The Temple was neutral territory bordering London in the north, but it wasn't part of the great city. The armed barons demanded that John confirm the charter of Henry I, but the king asked for a delay instead. The meeting was fruitless, and open war seemed a possibility in the near future.

The barons had the support of some of the bishops, as they swore to sustain the house of the Lord. They also promised to bring liberty to the church and to the whole realm. King John demanded that the barons swear fealty to him. He added a clause to the traditional oath of allegiance that asked his subjects to support him, not only against all men but also against the charter.

As the meeting in the new Temple reached a standstill, John and the barons agreed to delay and scheduled the next meeting to be held on April 26th. Both sides used this pause to make tactical decisions that would give them an advantage over the opposing side. To confirm his alliance with the pope, and to be certain he would receive support from the Vatican, John "took the cross." which means that he vowed to join the crusade. This vow secured his protection from the church on all matters, as the medieval ecclesiastical law dictated. Pope Innocent III took the opportunity to officially condemn the actions of the rebellious barons. He also ordered them to put down arms and swear an oath to the king, threatening excommunication for anyone who refused to do so. The Pope also wrote to Langton, accusing him of failing to act as a mediator and bring peace to the kingdom. Once again, he ordered Langton to persuade the two sides to agree with each other at all costs.

As the day of the next meeting with the king approached, the barons gathered their armed forces at Stamford. They started their march towards Northampton, the location where the meeting was to take place. On route, they were joined by Robert Fitzwalter and Geoffrey Mandeville, Earl of Essex, accompanied by their own forces. The barons' army grew as they approached Northampton, becoming a substantial force that threatened the king. John, however, broke his word yet again. He did not come to the appointed meeting. Instead, he promised safe passage to anyone who would come to him to talk through the mediation of Archbishop Langton. The barons continued their march and met with Langton at Brackley, a manor belonging to the Earl of Winchester. There the barons drew up a list of demands they had for the king and presented it to Langton. This list would serve as the basis for the Magna Carta, and Langton made sure John would receive it. Upon hearing the demands, John immediately denounced them, saying that the barons were vain and unreasonable. He also said that if he granted them all the liberties they ask for, it would mean the king would become their slave, not their ruler.

The barons were given no other choice but to carry out their threat of civil war. They renounced their oaths of allegiance to the king on May 5ᵗʰ. Robert Fitzwalter became the commander-in-chief of the rebellion, and he took the title Marshal of the Army of God and the Holy Church in pure defiance of John's taking on the cross and his alliance with the Vatican. Their first goal was to lay siege to the castle at Northampton, the king's own property. There, the rebels faced their first losses. Many died in the fruitless siege, as they did not have any siege engines. Not wanting to lose even more people, the barons decided to give up on the Northampton Castle and instead continue their march to Bedford.

On May 9ᵗʰ, John issued a charter referring to all the demands of the rebelling barons. He promised the pope would act as chairman of the new commission made of eight barons, four of whom would be chosen from those who remained loyal to the king, and four of whom would be chosen by the rebels from amongst their own ranks. On May 10ᵗʰ, he promised free passage to the rebel barons without repercussions. Furthermore, he promised he would not arrest or attack the barons. However, only two days later, John issued an order allowing his men to seize the lands owned by the rebelling barons.

Using the opportunity of May 9ᵗʰ and John's charter, by which he promised to deal with all the demands of the rebels, the barons drew up a document that historians refer to as the "Unknown Charter of Liberties." Once again, the new charter was built on Henry's Charter of Liberties—using seven clauses directly from it—with new ones that had the purpose of reinforcing those existing liberties. King John tried to buy more time hoping that Pope Innocent III would back him up. However, the rebel barons did not find his delays appropriate. They could not lose momentum, so they decided to gather an army and attack London. In reply, John tried to gain the support of the citizens of London by issuing a special charter that would grant them certain rights and the ability to elect a new mayor every year. But Robert Fitzwalter had his own ties to London. As the lord of Baynard's Castle, he acted as the procurator of the city, a standard-bearer, and the commander of the city militia. Other than these official titles, he also had trade ties in London which granted him access to all classes of the population. Using his web of contacts and favors, Fitzwalter managed to secure the support of London's citizens for the rebelling barons. When the army arrived in London on May 17th, the gates of the city were open for them, and they took control of the city without any resistance.

Even though London was practically granted to them, Fitzwalter and the other barons decided to attack the Jews, demolish their houses, and use the materials to reinforce the city walls. The barons who continued to support the king were not spared, either. Their property was plundered and used to finance the cause, and their houses were burned down, demolished, or repurposed. The fall of the capital city was decisive. Many barons who were loyalists decided to join the rebellion—some out of fear for their lives and properties, others realizing where the political power lay. Only a few barons chose to resist, and they had to flee the city to continue supporting the king.

John was forced to agree on a truce, and he sent out his men to act as intermediaries on May 27th. He took up residence in Windsor Castle, where he remained during the negotiations. With the king in Windsor and the rebelling barons in Staines on The River Thames, there was only one place that was convenient for the meeting between the two conflicting parties: Runnymede. This place was a meadow on the south bank of the Thames, situated midway from Windsor and Staines. Because both parties came with armed forces behind them, any meeting place could easily become a battlefield. Runnymede was chosen because the ground was too wet and boggy; therefore, nobody would be mad enough to start a battle there.

Accompanied by Stephen Langton, King John came in person to meet the barons at Runnymede on July 10th. This was the date he set his seal on the peace treaty that contained all the terms the barons demanded. This document historians call the Articles of the Barons, as it is titled: "These are the Articles which the barons seek and which the king agrees."[1] Over the course of the next ten days, Stephen Langton managed to convert the articles into a charter. As an extraordinary peace mediator, Langton had to fulfill the demands of the barons and turn them into a peace proposal. When King John finally accepted the proposed treaty, he placed his seal on it as a

---

[1] The Article of the Barons. (2014, September 15). Retrieved from https://www.bl.uk/collection-items/the-articles-of-the-barons

symbol of agreement. The seal was the standard double-sided great seal of England, and it was attached to the document at the bottom using cords.

The seal of the Angevin dynasty was a reference to the Old Testament text in which the Jews demand to have a king: "...that our king may judge us, and go out before us and fight our battles."[2] On one side of the royal seal was a visual representation of a king as a judge, and on the other side was the image of a king as a military commander. It is ironic that John, a king who failed his nation in both instances—as a judge and as a battle commander—used this seal. History remembers him only as an unjust judge and an unsuccessful military leader who lost all of England's continental territories. Furthermore, the seal was now being used to surrender royal power rather than to enhance it, as it had in the past.

The document which was sealed at Runnymede was indeed The Great Charter, or Magna Carta. but it wouldn't be called by that name for a few more years. No matter what name was used at the time, the document was a symbol of the fast-changing politics of the 13th century and indicated the decline of royal power. Unlike the "Unknown Charter," which had only twelve articles, the Articles of the Barons had forty-eight. Amongst them was an article that granted liberties to the city of London, such as the freedom of trade and transportation on River Thames. The citizens of London did well by siding with the barons since their decision brought nothing but advantages to the city.

Even though Robert Fitzwalter took the title "Marshal of the Army of God and Holy Church," it is rather unusual that the Articles of the Barons do not contain a single article that refers to the rights of the church. It is clear that the Articles tried to exclude the pope from English politics, and it is rather strange that King John agreed. The last article indeed says that the king has no right to ask the pope to revoke or diminish this document in any way. And even if he would try to do so, the document is secured, as no agreement of such nature between the king and the pope would be recognized by the law.

---

[2] Bible, Samuel 8,20

The distrust that the barons displayed for the king continued as they insisted on taking the Articles to London themselves. In fact, some of the barons did not find it satisfactory enough that the document was sealed by the king. They wanted even more proof of the king's goodwill. Therefore, Stephen Langton and other bishops of England, together with the papal legate Pandulf, were responsible for the king's behavior. They were tasked with securing the king's respect for the articles.

On June 15th, another plenary session was held at Runnymede. This date is celebrated in England as a historically important day when the Magna Carta was signed. The event is represented in English culture by various sculptors, painters, and writers. Politicians throughout history have used this event for their campaigns. Many tried to install the date as another bank holiday, a national public holiday in the United Kingdom. Even though the popular opinion is that the Magna Carta was signed on June 15th, there is no evidence to confirm this claim. Except for one contemporary writer's mention that a meeting was held at Runnymede on this date, there is no evidence to confirm what this meeting was about. It could not have been the signing for plenty of reasons: King John could not write, and in Medieval England, documents were acknowledged with a seal, not a manual signature. It is already known that the king sealed the Articles on June 10th. However, in medieval times, rulers would not stoop so low as to seal their own documents. For this purpose, there was a selected member of the Court of Chancery called a spigurnel, whose duty was to seal documents with the king's approval. History can only guess what happened on this date and if June 15th is the right date, as only one unknown writer mentions it.

It is generally believed that the concluding clause, numbered sixty-three, was added during the meeting on June 15th. This clause calls for the liberation of the church and reminds of the liberties and rights of citizens and their heirs:

"Wherefore we wish and firmly enjoin that the English church shall be free,

and that the men in our kingdom shall have and hold all the aforesaid

liberties, rights and concessions well and peacefully, freely and quietly, fully and completely, for themselves and their heirs from us and our heirs,

in all matters and in all places for ever, as is aforesaid. An oath, moreover,

has been taken, as well on our part as on the part of barons, that all these

things aforesaid shall be observed in good faith and without evil dispositions."[3]

This section from the Magna Carta can be treated as a clue to what happened on June 15th. It wasn't the signing of the Great Charter, as it is commonly believed, but rather the proclamation, conclusion, and promise of an oath.

The satisfied barons renewed their oaths of allegiance to the king four days later, on June 19th. The ceremony was rich, and the king wore the regalia of his grandmother, Empress Matilda. With the Great Charter to ensure their rights, the barons were eager to swear fealty to their king. Contemporary writers agree there was no sign of animosity between the once-angry barons and King John during the oath-renewing ceremony, which took place at Runnymede.

In the period between June 10th and June 15th, even more articles were added to the Charter. Especially important is Clause 14, which describes the "common council" of the kingdom. The vague phrase "common council" was neatly defined as a summoned parliament-like assembly of barons, bishops, and major landlords who were now given the power to decide if new taxes were valid, justified, and of a reasonable amount.

---

[3] Magna Carta, Clause 63

Chapter 3 – The Magna Carta

The 1215 Magna Carta written in Medieval Latin

(Source:
https://en.wikipedia.org/wiki/Magna_Carta#/media/File:Magna_Carta_(British_Libr
ary_Cotton_MS_Augustus_II.106).jpg)

The Magna Carta was written in Latin and in prose. It was only later, in modern times, that it was divided into sixty-three clauses that appear to be a collection of statements that follow each other without any obvious order. However, when it is read in prose, it becomes an obvious critique of the rule of the Plantagenets, particularly John. The Magna Carta deals with political, legal, economic, ecclesiastical, and feudal matters—all of which were of great importance then and remain of great importance today, as well.

The document begins with a preamble, or introduction, in which King John addresses all the men of his kingdom. He retains, in this document, the titles Duke of Normandy, Duke of Aquitaine, and Count of Anjou, even though he lost those territories much earlier during his reign. The men he is addressing are listed as archbishops, bishops, abbots, barons, and earls, but he also names his servants: foresters, justices, sheriffs, reeves, and others. The most important part of the address is that it finishes with *omnibus fidelibus suis*, which translates to "all the faithful ones." By this, John made it known that the Great Charter was not granted to those who were not his loyal subjects. The Charter wasn't given freely, from the king to the people. It was valid only for those who would renew their oaths and swear fealty to the king. Only those who were faithful to the Crown had the right to enjoy the freedoms and peace guaranteed by the Magna Carta.

The document continues with a list of the king's advisors. There are twenty-seven names of people who worked on the Magna Carta. Most of them were bishops and barons who remained loyal to the king during the barons' revolt. These same names are repeated in Clause 62, where they are listed as witnesses to the document. As the prime mediator of the Magna Carta at Runnymede and even before, Stephen Langton is at the top of the list. He is described as "Primate of all England and Cardinal of the Holy Roman Church." No doubt, under his influence, the first clause of the Magna Carta deals with the status of the church.

The first words of the first clause in the Magna Carta are as follows: "Firstly, we have granted to God and confirmed by this, our present charter, for us and our heirs in perpetuity, that the English Church shall be free."[4]

It is commonly believed that this was Langton's attempt to, once and for all, deal with the issue that raged between the Plantagenet kings and the church since the 1160s when Henry II clashed with Thomas Becket. This first line that regards the church and its status is an echo of the opening remarks of Henry I's Coronation Charter, which had a prime influence on the Magna Carta. Langton managed to secure the fact that the king had no right to interfere in church elections. Perhaps his personal experience, when John refused to recognize him as Archbishop of Canterbury, gave him the motivation to fight for this cause specifically. Aside from being the first clause, there is another important aspect of this clause that describes the church and its liberties. After this clause ends, the king re-introduces the Great Charter with the following statement: "We have also granted to all the freemen of our realm ..." [5]This new start gives special

---

[4] Magna Carta Translation, Clause 1. (n.d.). Retrieved from https://www.archives.gov/exhibits/featured-documents/magna-carta/translation.html

[5] Magna Carta Translation, re-introduction. (n.d.). Retrieved from https://www.archives.gov/exhibits/featured-documents/magna-carta/translation.html

importance to the clause that refers to the church. It is not only the first promise but also a separate promise to the church. As such, it is placed above all other promises the king made in the Magna Carta, which lead some historians to believe that the church enjoyed special protection.

The barons did not include the church in their articles when they first proposed such a document. However, the Magna Carta does refer to the English church. In fact, it placed the church above all else. Even though Langton came late to the negotiations, he managed to lift his own political interests to the top. As if to affirm the special status the church was given in this document, Clause 63 states the following: "We wish and firmly command that the English church shall be free and that men in our kingdom have and hold all the aforesaid liberties." [6]While the first draft of the Magna Carta in the form of the Barons' Articles was a secular document, the Magna Carta is not. In it, religious considerations take precedence and are treated separately from the rest of the document.

The next issue the Magna Carta dealt with was the most important one for the barons: the rights and reliefs of inheritance. In the second article, John promised that he would limit the royal inheritance fee to £100, and it would be equal for all earls, barons, and other great men of importance. The fee was lowered to 100 marks in the case of knights. As a side note, the mark in Medieval England wasn't a coin but a unit of accounting introduced by the Danes. One mark was worth thirteen shillings and fourpence.

Consequently, the king would not charge outrageous amounts of money for the right to inherit lands and properties. Cases such as that of William FitzAlan, who was charged £10,000 to receive his inheritance, would not repeat. Through other clauses, the king promised he would not force his men into bankruptcy to retain political control over them. He would not seize land or other properties for a debt if the debtor could repay with his personal possessions. The process of determining the wealth of a deceased person was given in detail. Exchequers had no right to extort, bully,

[6] Magna Carta Translation, Clause 63. (n.d.). Retrieved from https://www.archives.gov/exhibits/featured-documents/magna-carta/translation.html

and ruin people, and they were placed under strict supervision (Clause 26 and 27).

Other clauses of the Magna Carta referred to various aspects of the law of inheritance. Widows did not pay the inheritance fee to the king and were given access to their portion of the property immediately after the death of their husbands. Clauses 7 and 8 also made sure widows would not be married again against their will. However, this does not mean that the Magna Carta was liberal when it came to the rights of women. For example, Clause 54 states: "No man shall be arrested or imprisoned because of the appeal of a woman for the death of anyone but her husband." [7]

Clause 3 states that young men who were not yet of the legal age of maturity would not be forced to pay the king's fee for an inheritance but would be able to inherit their possessions only when they reached the legal age of adulthood. Under Clause 37, young men were protected from the king's will to seize them and claim them as his wards. Anyone who was granted the wardship of minors was to be respectful of his inheritance and not use it for personal gain.

Clauses 10 and 11 of the Magna Carta dealt with debts to Jewish moneylenders and to the king, who was forbidden from pursuing high-interest loans through his own officials. Clause 13 confirms London's ancient liberties, as it was the city that played a key role in the negotiations between the king and the revolting barons. The merchants who inhabited London were given freedom of movement, both on land and on water. They were also exempted from the "evil tolls." The same clause then describes how foreign merchants should be treated during times of war.

People seeking justice now had the Court of Common Pleas, which had a fixed location. Until the Magna Carta, the citizens of the kingdom had to find John and ask for an audience. Magna Carta guaranteed county courts would be held at a fixed time and at a fixed place throughout the year, and the fines for offenses were to be within reasonable amounts (Clauses 17-22).

---

[7] Magna Carta Translation, Clause 54. (n.d.). Retrieved from https://www.archives.gov/exhibits/featured-documents/magna-carta/translation.html

Clause 35 of the Magna Carta regulated measures for all the important things in the kingdom, such as corn, cloth, ale, and grain. Purveyance was banned by the document, which meant that royal officials could no longer confiscate goods, grain, or horses for the king's personal use. If the king was in immediate need of such things, his officials had to pay for them.

Clause 44 concerned the people who lived outside the forest lands and protected them from being judged by forest law. Clauses 47 and 48 touched on the forest law, as well, limiting the boundaries of the forest and urging the investigation of corruption among forest officials.

The Magna Carta dealt with common law but also with grand ideas. It is no wonder some of its clauses were used for over eight centuries. For example, Clause 21 states that barons and earls could be fined only by their peers and "in accordance with the offense."[8] Another clause that was long-lived is Clause 45. It says: "Judges, sheriffs, and other royal officials are to be competent." Later, Clause 39 was expanded and became one of the most enduring and relevant statements of any constitutional document. Its final shape is as follows:

"No free man is to be arrested, or imprisoned or disseized, or outlawed, or exiled, or in any other way ruined, nor will we go or send against him, except by the legal judgment of his peers or by the law of the land (*nisi per legale judicium parum sourum*)."[9]

There is no doubt that this clause was designed with the intention of stopping King John from legally pursuing some of his greatest men. Together with Clause 40, which simply says, "To no one will we sell, to no one will we deny or delay, right or justice," Clause 39 is the foundation of the principles of trial by jury. It also carries the basic idea that justice should always restrain the government from abusing its power.

The Magna Carta is a far-reaching document, yet much of it remains vague, and some areas of the Magna Carta seem unfinished.

---

[8]   Magna   Carta   Translation,   Clause   21.   (n.d.).   Retrieved   from https://www.archives.gov/exhibits/featured-documents/magna-carta/translation.html

[9]   Magna   Carta   Translation,   Clause   39.   (n.d.).   Retrieved   from https://www.archives.gov/exhibits/featured-documents/magna-carta/translation.html

Some clauses were clearly intended to push some of the complex political issues of the time; however, they feel rushed or abandoned mid-sentence. For example, Clauses 49, 50, and 51 speak of the king's promise to release all hostages and give charters to the people of England as security of peace. He also promised he would expel foreign knights and mercenary soldiers; however, there are no details as to when and where this would happen. These clauses seem like the beginning of an idea, but much is left unspoken.

Clauses 39 and 40 are, to this day, considered the foundations of modern Western democracy, but Clause 61 is of equal importance. It is known as the "security clause" by which men who lived in 1215 found a way to hold the king to his word given in the Great Charter. Without it, the king was free to break his promises to the people and return to his old ways of rule. The security clause speaks of a possible scenario where, if the king was to "transgress against any of the articles of the peace ...", a council of twenty-five barons was under the full right to "distrain upon and distress us in all ways possible, by taking castles, lands and possessions and in any other ways they can ... saving our person and the persons of our queen and children." [10] This meant that if the king broke his promises, he would have to face the wrath of his own subjects. The Magna Carta made civil war legal, which is rather strange for a document that was to ensure peace.

There are only four parchment versions of the Magna Carta that survive to this day. Two of them are held in the British Library (of which one is badly damaged by a fire that occurred in 1731), the third is secured in the Salisbury Cathedral, and the fourth is kept in Lincoln Castle. There are variations among these four documents, but they are all replicas of the agreement. They all bear a stamp of authenticity, a double-sided wax royal seal attached to the bottom of the documents with a short silk cord. There were many more copies of the Magna Carta, and many copies and reissues survived in archives around the world, but only these four documents are considered the "original" charters. It is unknown if there was ever one original document from which all the copies were made or if the copies were made

---

[10] Magna Carta Translation, Clause 61. (n.d.). Retrieved from https://www.archives.gov/exhibits/featured-documents/magna-carta/translation.html

simultaneously. The signing of the Magna Carta is often depicted romantically, with the king ceremonially signing the document, but as discussed above, that probably never happened. Many of the events that surround the creation of the Magna Carta remain a mystery. History can only guess how the process of turning a peace agreement into a document with constitutional principles took place, and it took a long time to finish.

Chapter 4 – The Failure of the Magna Carta

History often places the blame for the failure of the Magna Carta solely on King John. Although he is not without blame, the barons weren't saints either. They quickly started abusing their newly gained power, similarly to John at his worst. The barons were aware that John would try to wiggle out of the Great Charter, considering his systematic dishonesty in the past. The barons were determined to stop him. The already mentioned Clause 61 gave the barons the much-needed liberty to act if the king was breaking his promises. This clause was solely the work of the barons, as it came directly from the Articles of the Barons, and was not changed by the royal clerks, as other articles were. The barons did not trust anyone, and they took it upon themselves to write Clause 61 in detail and in full so that it wouldn't be tampered with. The article was written in a long paragraph of continuous prose.

Clause 61 begins this way: "This is the *forma securitatis* [formula, or terms of security] for the preservation of the peace and liberties between the king and the kingdom." [11] As mentioned in the previous chapter, this clause sets up the council, or panel, of twenty-five barons, chosen by the baronage. The council had far-reaching powers that were to be used to "... observe, maintain and cause to be observed the peace and liberties which we have granted." [12] If the articles of the Great Charter were not respected by the king or his officials, the four barons of the council were to be informed. These four had the power to conduct their own investigation, which would confirm a possible breach of the Charter. If the breach was not rectified within forty days of its committing, the four barons would be obliged to notify the council of twenty-five. The council was then to punish the king until, in their own judgment, the king made amends. The *forma securitatis*

---

[11] Magna Carta Translation, Clause 61. (n.d.). Retrieved from https://www.archives.gov/exhibits/featured-documents/magna-carta/translation.html

[12] Magna Carta Translation, Clause 61. (n.d.). Retrieved from https://www.archives.gov/exhibits/featured-documents/magna-carta/translation.html

promised the barons great power, which was to be used to limit the king. Nothing was off-limits to the barons except hurting the king, queen, and their children.

Every citizen had to obey and assist the twenty-five in their judgment and actions. Some barons were even empowered to act on behalf of the whole council, as they had the role of overruling the absent or dissenter barons. The twenty-five were meant to represent public safety. They were a self-recruited and permanent committee, which probably had the intention of becoming an aristocratic oligarchy if given enough time. If allowed, they would turn England into something like the Republic of Venice, where the king was just a puppet to his aristocratic rulers. However, the twenty-five never lived long enough as a political entity to reach their goals. Still, they had an immediate role to play.

As soon as the Magna Carta was ratified, the council of barons took it upon themselves to correct all the king's wrongs. They had among their ranks many of the barons who were casualties of King John's rule. They were to judge each separate case and demand compensation. Furthermore, they had the right to assert the extent of the compensation the king had to pay—be it with money, lands and castles, or other possessions. The twenty-five went so far as to use their newfound power to humiliate John, their former oppressor. Clause 61, the famous *forma securitatis*, clearly states that the four who were to represent and investigate the case should "come to Us," meaning they were supposed to go to the king to state their case. However, the barons considered this task beneath their dignity, so they demanded that the king come to them. In fact, while King John was sick with gout and in bed, they refused to come to his chambers or even excuse the king's presence. King John had to be carried on a litter in front of the twenty-five, who then proceeded to judge him. The barons were intentionally showing off their power. It was a calculated move since King John had to comply. He was in a rush to conclude the cases, and fifty of the disputes were solved within the next ten days. During this time, twelve of the twenty-five panel members benefited greatly from the settled disputes. For instance, Richard de Clare received Buckingham, Robert Fitzwalter was given Hertford Castle, and Henry de Bohun came into possession of the manors of the honour of Trowbridge. However, King John did not simply agree with all the terms the barons placed in front of him. He occasionally protested and would not give in. But the barons would place him under such pressure that, by the end of the day, he would simply have to give in.

John was extremely weak after the Runnymede events. He lacked the respect of his subjects and had little to no power. On top of it all, he lost his capital city, London. The barons simply refused to give the city of London back to the king, even though they promised during the meeting at Runnymede to do so if the king would fulfill certain obligations. The Magna Carta itself did not deal with the issue of London. There is a separate document that records the agreement between the king and the barons on how to deal with the city. The document was titled "Convention," and it stated that if the king fulfilled special conditions, London would be given back to him on August 15, 1215. Until then, it was under the custody of Robert Fitzwalter and the panel of twenty-five barons. If the king failed to deliver his end of the deal, the city would remain in the custody of the barons. This agreement was written twice, and each party received their own copy. Only the copy that was in the king's possession survived and is kept in The National Archives. What is truly remarkable about this document is that it treats London as private property, and it also treats the king as a private person rather than the sovereign of a nation.

The terms of this document, classified as "indenture" were spelled out quite clearly. Local commissions of twelve knights were to investigate the local sheriffs and other royal officials and search for proof of violations of the forest law. The king's obligation was to meet all the claims against him and restore all the rights and properties of damaged individuals. The indenture gave only a two months' timeframe for this endeavor to be achieved. John had no other choice but to comply. After all, by doing what he was told, he could only gain back the trust of the English people, who might even give him their support once more. After the uprising and small civil war that happened before Runnymede, the population of England mostly stayed neutral. The king's loyalists were a minority, but the followers of the rebellious barons were a minority, too.

The political struggle to gain the favor of a large, neutral population began. While John started accepting his part of the promise, the barons organized tournaments and celebrations to entertain their army and gain even more followers. However, John did only half of what he was supposed to do and started claiming he won't do anything else unless the barons would give him something in return. He complained he was the only one working actively on peace while the barons did nothing. He asked them to make charters that would confirm their allegiance, but the barons refused to do so. Their refusal was exactly what the king hoped for, as it would give him political advantage. He was then able to create a picture of a benevolent king who was doing everything within his power to keep the peace, while the barons refused to keep their end of the deal.

The next meeting between King John and the barons was scheduled in Oxford on August 15th, a day after the expiration of the deadline given by the London indenture. The king did not show up in person. Instead, he sent a delegation to convey his message. They were instructed to say how the king had surrendered many things, as agreed, but had received nothing in return. The king continued to accuse the barons of causing him personal harm. He even went so far as to proclaim that he was afraid for his own life since the barons had gathered a large army. Smart enough, he did not call for the breakup of the Runnymede deal. He was simply complaining that the settlement achieved two months ago was not going forward as planned.

In return, the barons agreed to have yet another meeting with the king by the end of August. However, that meeting never happened, as it was right then when the barons learned that King John had already asked Rome to annul the Magna Carta. In fact, he had sent letters to Pope Innocent III back in May, on the very eve after the Runnymede meeting, complaining of the barons' behavior. By June 22nd, he sent another letter that asked Innocent III to annul the Great Charter. But in medieval times, it took months for letters to reach their destination, especially when traveling as far as Rome. The pope did not receive the news from England until November of 1215, and he was completely oblivious of the summer events between John and the barons.

Earlier that year, Innocent III had sent three letters to all involved parties in the English dispute: King John, the barons, and Langton—who, as you may remember, acted as a mediator and was supposed to resolve the conflict. His letters were written in the form of a sovereign addressing his subjects. Naturally, he expected Langton to do exactly as he was told, and the barons were expected to obey. Under the threat of excommunication, the barons were ordered to stop any violent treachery towards John and to regard the king with all the royal honors his title bore. When the pope received word from John that the barons had not listened to his instructions, he was furious. The barons had openly defied the pope, and Langton had not proceeded to excommunicate them. The Pope felt an obligation to teach them a lesson on obedience.

As a response, Innocent III issued a papal edict titled "*Mirari cogimur et moveri*" (We are compelled to wonder and be moved). In this bull (a type of public decree), the pope proclaimed King John to be innocent and a good Christian obedient to the church. Further, he mentioned Langton's failure to protect the king and accused him of conspiring with the rebellious barons. The Pope also accused the barons, whom he called "worse than Saracens,"[13] of trying to get rid of John and—by their actions—of preventing John from joining the holy war. Pope Innocent III took this opportunity to excommunicate the barons as well as their accomplices. He ordered the bishops and archbishops to proclaim the sentence of excommunication throughout England. He even threatened them with suspension if they decided to disobey.

Langton was stunned by the pope's letter. He saw himself as nothing more than a mediator who had tried to resolve the dispute between the king and the barons. However, the pope instructed him to abandon his neutrality and the role of a mediator. He was to openly take the king's side in the dispute. Langton had no choice, and he proceeded to obey the pope's orders. At the conference at Staines, in August, Langton excommunicated all who disturbed the peace in the kingdom, keeping the ceremony vague. He was not prepared to take

---

[13] *Selected Letters of Pope Innocent III concerning England (1198-1216)*, ed. C.R. Cheney and W. H. Semple (London, 1953) 196-7 no.75, from the dorse of the Patent Roll (*Mirari cogimur et moveri*, 19 March 1215).

the king's side, and he did not want to give up his neutrality. He also didn't want to excommunicate each one of the barons by name. Instead, the task fell to three commissioners whom the pope had already prepared in case Langton failed to do as instructed. They were Bishop of Winchester Peter des Roches, papal legate Pandulf, and the Abbot of Reading. On September 5th, the three published a letter specifying each baron's name and the deed for which they were being excommunicated. They also placed London under an interdict because the city had openly supported the barons during the civil war. Some of the clerical associates of the punished barons were also excommunicated, such as the Bishop of Hereford and the Archdeacon of Hereford.

Langton had been at the political center of English life ever since he was appointed to the position of Archbishop of Canterbury, and the Magna Carta crisis emphasized his role in politics. However, his failure to obey the pope's orders marked the immediate end of his political career. His refusal to name the barons who were excommunicated led to his suspension, as the pope had promised would happen to all who disobeyed.

In September, the Bishop of Winchester imposed Langton's penalty. In vain, Langton appealed to Rome. The pope only confirmed his suspension, deciding Langton should end his political and religious career in humiliation. Langton had to leave England, and at the same time as his departure, another letter from Pope Innocent arrived. In this letter, the pope denounced the Magna Carta, declared it dishonorable and shameful. He ordered John to break his oath to the Magna Carta by proclaiming it annulled and invalid. The Magna Carta was dead, and it achieved nothing for the short life it had. What followed was a civil war known as the First Barons' War.

Chapter 5 – The War

The Magna Carta was an ambitious peacemaking document, but it was also a great failure. The Great Charter failed to bind the king to his promises, and it failed to reconcile John to the northerners. Pope Innocent III annulled the document within months of its declaration, an act that brought back civil war and times of anarchy. In time, the Magna Carta would become one of the most revered documents in English history, but 1215 was not the year it happened.

It is unknown whether King John ever intended to stick to the terms presented in the Magna Carta. By July, he had probably abandoned such an idea, as he wrote to Pope Innocent III requesting the annulment of the document. In his letter, he claimed that the terms for the Magna Carta were extracted from him with threats of violence and, as such, were not binding. The pope was happy to agree, and by September 1215, he sent letters to England in which he expressed anger that John, a papal vassal, was treated so by his subjects. As John's superior, he had all the right to release the king from the obligations which the Magna Carta imposed on him. The English translation of Pope Innocent III's letter was printed in *English Historical Documents*, and it says the following: "Although our well-beloved son in Christ, John illustrious King of the English, grievously offended God and the Church ... the king at length returned to his senses ... But the enemy of the human race [Satan] who always hates good impulses, by his cunning wiles, stirred up against him the barons of England so that, with a wicked inconstancy, the men who supported him when injuring the Church rebelled against him when he turned from his sin. ..." The pope took a firm tone right from the beginning of his letters. Innocent III accused the barons of being unreasonable, treacherous, and aggressive. He accused the whole English nation of shameful actions that thwarted the plans for the crusade in the holy land. The pope finished his letters by stating: "We utterly reject and condemn this settlement and under threat of excommunication we order that the king should not dare to observe it and that the barons and their associates should not require it to be observed."[14] With these words, Pope Innocent III annulled the Magna

---

[14] English Historical Documents, Vol. III, op.cit., pp.324-6

Carta. He excommunicated nine barons and all the citizens of London who he openly blamed for the duress that King John had to endure.

The result of the Magna Carta's annulment was the resumption of civil war. It was clear to the barons that King John would not be reformed or controlled in any way. John's behavior turned out to be quite contrary to the barons' wishes. By September 17th, John returned to his habit of seizing baronial estates by force. It was no wonder his opponents started resisting his rule once again. They ignored royal officials and even went so far as to replace them with their own barons' men. They refused to pay the money owed to the Crown. The most drastic action John's opposition undertook was the development of plans to replace the king. John threatened Archbishop Langton, who refused to give up his Rochester Castle. The argument ended up with the siege of the castle, which had a vital strategical position. At the same time, this siege was also the first armed conflict that started the First Barons' War.

Rochester Castle sits on the Roman road known as Watling Street. This road was a lifeline for Britain. Armies used it to easily transport men, mercenaries, arms, and supplies from the continental territories to Dover, and then move them all over England. Rochester Castle was granted to the Archbishops of Canterbury by Henry I. This is how it, eventually, went into Langton's hands. John reached an agreement with the Archbishop that the castle would be returned to the royal house once the Magna Carta was signed, but Langton refused to give up the castle, trying to remain neutral in the conflict to the very end. At the end of September of 1215, when Langton had already left England, the castle was finally surrendered to the barons.

John occupied the castle on October 13th as a response to the barons who decided to station a garrison in Rochester. John's army was larger, and the barons never came to help defend their castle. The defenders at Rochester Castle managed to resist for five weeks before they were forced to surrender due to supply exhaustion.

The barons were bold enough to write letters to Louis the Lion, a French prince and son of Philip Augustus. They invited him to join their cause, invade England, and take the crown for himself. The northern barons invited Alexander II of the Scots to invade

Northumbria, Westmorland, and Cumberland. In Wales, Llywelyn ap Iorwerth (Llywelyn the Great) proclaimed himself a prince and captured all English-held castles in his territory. By December, a party of French knights arrived in London. John had to divide his attention to face possible attacks from three foreign princes as well as his subjects.

John finally began to feel the pressure the barons were putting on his hold of England, and his power began to weaken. He decided the north caused the most trouble, and he went to deal with the situation in the borderlands. The town of Berwick was the first to fall to John in the first days of 1216. To show off his power, John decided to burn the town, hoping it would be enough to scare off his enemies. His whole campaign in the north was designed to intimidate and bring terror to his subjects. He wanted to make sure they would realize he was still a king and had all the power over them. He continued to destroy and burn villages and farms. He allowed his soldiers, who were mostly mercenaries, to rape, murder, and steal. John also forced men to pay money for their and their families' freedom, as he was in constant need of money to finance his army.

The campaign against the Scots in the north was a success, and King John now turned toward the southeast. He brutalized Lincoln and Fotheringay on his way to East Anglia and Essex before turning west toward Oxford. He made the defeated rebels swear an oath to renounce the Magna Carta. People were afraid of his army, and resistance started to weaken. Some barons decided to turn their castles over to John without resistance just at the sight of his army. By March 1216, the barons started considering peace with John and probably would have given in if a rumor about Louis preparing to set sail for England had not started to circulate in April. Even John started preparing for a French invasion, fortifying the coast around Kent and sending his fleet across the Channel. The fleet's task was to try to block Louis in port and prevent him from even setting sail. However, they were unsuccessful, and the French prince landed in England at the end of May. At the sight of French sails, John decided to retreat to Winchester. Louis led his army through Kent toward London, where he was greeted with much cheer on June 2nd. There, he made a promise to restore all the old English laws and rule as a just king, while Fitzwalter and Mayor William Handel led the rebels and the London citizens to pay homage to Louis and admit him as their sovereign. Only four days later, Louis took upon himself the task of pursuing John.

The French prince proved to be worthy of his nickname "Louis the Lion" due to not only his military successes but also his political prowess. He didn't bring just his army from France. He came with carefully prepared propaganda, the author of which was probably Simon Langton, brother to Stephen Langton and Louis' chancellor. It is well known that Simon joined Louis in his invasion of England, helping him craft his claim to the throne. He claimed a hereditary right to the realm of England because his wife was Blanche, daughter of Queen Eleanor of Castile, who was the sister of Richard the Lionheart. He also claimed John lost his right to the throne when he betrayed his brother Richard while he was fighting in the crusade.

The second part of Louis' propaganda claimed he was elected to be king of England. Here, Louis called on the Charter, by which allegiance to the king was not legally given; it was a contract between the people and the king—a contract King John broke the first time when he handed England to Pope Innocent III without the consent of the barons. The second time John broke this contract was when he refused to comply with the Magna Carta and returned to his misgovernment. Louis stated that, given the circumstances, the barons had no other choice but to offer the crown to him.

Interestingly, Louis never promised to bring back the Magna Carta, only the old laws of England. And the barons did not seem to care. They still gave him their full support. This might mean that the barons didn't care about the Magna Carta itself and that John and Innocent III were somewhat right to denounce it. What the barons cared about most was their power, and it was of little interest to them how they would gain that power—be it through the Magna Carta or through a puppet king, such as Louis seemed to agree to be. It also might be that the barons—especially Fitzwalter and his cousin de Quincy—were so desperate to get rid of John, they simply didn't bother to name the terms when they invited the French prince to take the English crown.

The barons who were previously loyal to John started defecting. Even the new papal legate, Guala Bicchieri, was unable to fortify John's cause. Among the defecting barons was John's half-brother

William Longspée, Earl of Salisbury. John's army was weakened, and Louis managed to push him out of southeastern England. Encouraged by the events in England, the Scots attacked the borders once more and besieged some of the northern castles. Anarchy took over the country while the battle between the two kings, Louis of France and John of England, continued.

King John was powerless and decided to retreat to his favorite residence, Corfe Castle, while Louis was advancing through England undisturbed. The French prince besieged Winchester, a castle that managed to hold only for ten days. They sent word to John of their inability to resist the siege, and John permitted them to surrender. Winchester was considered the second capital of England, and it was shameful to surrender it without a fight. The second wave of defection followed. Disappointed by King John's cowardice, some of his loyalists abandoned him, joining forces with Louis. Over two-thirds of the loyal barons left the king and chose to either join the rebels or stay neutral and avoid the conflict. The barons weren't the only ones who changed sides. Two-thirds of John's knights left, as well as the royal administrators and some of his household.

Louis now held most of the country, while King John was left with only three castles to give resistance to the French invader: Dover, Lincoln, and Windsor. Soon, even these three castles were under siege. It was then that John decided to put up a resistance. He marched northeast toward his garrison in Lincoln, where he hoped to meet Alexander of the Scots and punish him for giving his allegiance to Louis. However, Alexander wasn't there, and John had to satisfy himself by burning and looting Cambridgeshire to punish East Anglia for giving support to the rebellious barons.

It seemed that the war would be long and merciless, as John expected help from his ally the Pope. However, in October of 1216, Pope Innocent III died. This was an event that influenced the war in England to its core. John was disappointed his protector and ally was suddenly out of the game. He could not rely on Rome's help anymore. On top of that, he received word that the Castle in Dover, his main stronghold in the battle against the French, could not endure the siege for much longer.

While staying in Norfolk, John fell ill with dysentery. The illness did not stop him from pushing his army forward, however. On October 12ᵗʰ, he urged his troops across the Wellstream River without thinking of the territory's conditions. The tide was not in far enough, and much of his army's rations, horses, and some men were swallowed by quicksand. Among the lost items were royal treasures, such as John's coronation regalia—items forever lost to history, never to be seen again.

John escaped the quicksand safely, but he was ill and furious. His illness was treated with ripe peaches and new cider which, by today's standards of medicine, could only worsen his symptoms. He pushed his court to continue traveling, but he was in such agony he had to be carried. The procession reached Newark, where John would die on October 18ᵗʰ. Before he died, he was persuaded to forgive his enemies. John had enough loyalists remaining by his side to fulfill his dying wish to bury him in Worcester, next to the shrine of St. Wulfstan.

Chapter 6 – The Regent and the End of the First Barons' War

When King John died, his son and heir was only nine years old. To help him ascend to the throne in a war-torn country, John appointed a council of thirteen executors whose task was to guide King Henry III in his rule and help him regain his kingdom. A minor ascending the throne in the medieval world was often disastrous, as a child was an easy target to the political opponents of the current regime. Age was not the only problem Henry III had to face at the start of his rule. More than half of England was under foreign rule, which had the support of most of the aristocracy. Under such circumstances, it is amazing that Henry III defied all expectations and managed to not only claim the throne but also thrive as a ruler. Henry's accession saved the House of Anjou, the kingdom, and the Great Charter. But it wasn't the child-king who was to be thanked for it. Largely, Henry III owed everything he was and everything he possessed to the Earl of Pembroke, William Marshal, appointed by John himself to be Henry's guardian.

William Marshal, one of the most famous knights of England, was seventy years old when he took on the role of caretaker for young Henry III. Marshal was the younger son of a minor nobleman; therefore, he had no lands or fortune and had to fight his way through life. He began training as a knight in Normandy, at a court of his cousin, William de Tancarville. Contrary to popular belief, studying for knighthood involved learning Biblical history, Latin, and the politics of the courts. William was knighted in 1166 during the campaign in Normandy, which was invaded by Flanders. The very next year, he tried the tournament for the first time, and there he found his true calling. William Marshal was tall, handsome, and strong, and as such, he easily became a star in tournaments. His martial skills with the lance and sword brought him international fame, money, and a very wealthy wife later in life. It also opened the doors of the Angevine court to him. He was a part of Queen Eleanor's escort when she was ambushed. Although the queen managed to escape, young William was caught and taken as a prisoner. Hearing of his bravery, Queen Eleanor paid for his ransom and once more employed him in her service, from where he was later transferred to serve as a combat tutor to young Henry III. Together, the young king and Marshal traveled Europe joining various tournaments. Even though later William was accused of having an affair with the king's wife, the friendship between the two remained strong, and Henry would ask for William on his deathbed. After the death of the young king, William Marshal joined the crusade and traveled to Jerusalem, but nothing is known of his deeds there.

William was forty-three when he married the seventeen-year-old daughter of Richard de Clare, Earl of Pembroke. Marshal suddenly had a claim over the large estates in England, most notably Wales and Ireland, as well as in Normandy. This marriage transformed William from a landless knight and son of a minor noble to one of the richest men in England who would become the Earl of Pembroke after his father-in-law's death. During the reign of Richard, John's older brother, William was in the king's service and supported him during the war in Normandy against Philip II of France. When John became the king in 1199, William offered him his services and proved to be loyal to the Crown. Even though his relationship with John cooled of and even escalated to outright hostility at one point, William Marshal stayed loyal to King John during his initial conflict with the barons. During the meeting at Runnymede where the Magna Carta was signed, Marshal supported the king, and he stayed loyal through the First Barons' War. His name is often mentioned as the leading negotiator between the king and the barons. William is also listed as the first of the noblemen who advised the king concerning the Magna Carta at Runnymede. His loyalty to the Crown was probably most displayed when he took responsibility for the funeral of the much-hated King John.

Interestingly, John is the first English king who left a testament behind him. This document was hurried, and it contained only sixteen lines, as John was aware he had no time to deal with all his possessions. The testament mostly deals with the salvation of the king's soul. Churches were to receive donations to repair the injuries they had endured by the king's hand. He also rewarded his faithful servants and specified the distribution of alms for the poor. His testament also contained instructions on how and where to bury him. The rest was left to his administrators to deal with as they saw fit. In the end, the document contained the names of thirteen councilors who were to help his son restore the kingdom. Two prominent names stood out: Cardinal Guala Bicchieri was named leader of the churchmen whose names were on the list, and William Marshal was named leader of the nobles who were chosen as councilors.

William Marshal was named not only the protector of the boy-king Henry III but also the regent of England—or at least this is what history leads us to believe. The only source of this information is a biographer of William Marshal, who may have been biased due to the personal nature of the topic. Although some historians are eager to dispute that Marshal was named regent, it is a plausible event. He was already one of the richest men in the kingdom and had great influence in court and generally in politics. Besides, he was the pillar of John's regime. To secure the success of the dynasty, who would have been a better choice than the chivalrous knight William Marshal?

Marshal rushed Henry III's coronation, as the political scene of England was uncertain. He hoped to gain a foothold with the ceremony, so only ten days after John's death, on October 28th, Henry III was crowned at Gloucester. The very next day, the council of thirteen gathered, where Marshal begged to be excused from the role of regent, due to his advanced age. The second choice for a regent was Earl Ranulf de Blondeville, who raised objections to his qualifications and praised Marshal as the only suitable candidate. The new papal legate, Guala Bicchieri, promised William absolution from all his sins, and it seems this was the act that convinced the old Earl of Pembroke to accept the regency.

Guala was sent to England as the new papal legate of Innocent III, who died only a few months later. His role was to protect John and Rome's interests in England. With the new pope, Honorius III, and the new king of England, Henry III, the politics between these two sides did not change. The pope was still the overlord of England, and the young king had to pay him homage and acknowledge him as his superior. Guala was an enthusiastic enforcer of these politics, and his first act as papal legate was to excommunicate Prince Louis and his associates who helped him in the invasion of England. With William Marshal as regent, Guala was even more certain of his actions, and he went so far as to call for a crusade against Louis, uniting the church and the state into a common cause against the French.

On November 12, 1216, William Marshal and the council of thirteen advised the young King Henry III to reissue the Magna Carta. However, it was the Magna Carta transformed. First to suffer transformation was Clause 61, the famous *forma securitatis*. After all, it was the clause that went against everything the loyalists and the pope stood for. In it, the Great Charter was described as more important than an oath to a king. Furthermore, it gave immense power to the panel of twenty-five barons, who were supposed to act as bringers of justice and whose goal was to elevate the king into a role like that of the Venetian doge.

Next to be transformed was Clause 48, which commissioned twelve knights to investigate John's forest law. The problem the knights presented for the new king was their ability to transform into a powerful entity, like the panel of twenty-five but on a local level. The power they could gain posed a threat to the stability of the Crown. Clauses that required the king to compensate immediately for all the misgovernment of John's rule had to be removed. Others were labeled as important, but to be considered later. The core of the Great Charter was left intact. Feudal incidents were to be settled according to the Magna Carta, justice administration was to be reformed, weights and measures were to be standardized, and trade was given guaranteed freedom. The core of the Magna Carta became the new law, with improvements and clarifications in places that needed it.

Since all of John's regalia was kept in Winchester, which was still occupied by the enemies of the Crown, Henry III had no seals with which to declare the Great Charter. Instead, it was Guala who sealed the document as a representative of the pope, the king's superior. This meant that the pope himself endorsed the reissued Charter, even though Rome annulled it in its previous form. What changed so significantly that the pope suddenly accepted the Charter? It wasn't just its transformation to better suit the king. It was also a convenient thing to do since Louis himself failed to commit to the Magna Carta or to reissue it. The people also believed in the revised Charter, and the proof for that is the fact that William Marshal sent copies to

Ireland, where the twenty-five had no power. Ireland stayed loyal to John in his struggles against the barons. The reissued Magna Carta was a proper basis on which to rebuild the royal government once Louis was dealt with. They also hoped the new Charter would appease the barons, who would once again swear fealty to the Crown.

The newly-transformed Magna Carta did not manage to bring back the barons. They did not offer their support to Henry, as William Marshal hoped they would. The king's opposition hardened. But Louis could not be officially crowned a king, even though Westminster Abbey was under his control. Henry was the one who had the support of the pope and the English church. Despite this, William Marshal had to deal with several months of political stalemate. War campaigns were usually suspended during the winter, and this one was no different. In February of 1217, Louis departed England in hopes of bringing reinforcements from France. While Louis was away, the barons were garrisoned in London once more. To pass the time while waiting for the French reinforcements, the barons decided to organize a tournament. However, the tournament gained a voice of its own, and the knights, barons, and army embarked on a journey through the English midlands to attempt to free Mountsorrel Castle in Leicestershire. This castle belonged to none other than Saer de Quincy, 1ˢᵗ Earl of Winchester and cousin to Robert Fitzwalter. It was also occupied by the royalists at the time of the tournament. Louis returned to England just in time to join the endeavor in Leicestershire, bringing the army from France. In total, there were around six hundred knights and one thousand footmen. Saer de Quincy personally led the English army joined by Fitzwalter, while the French troops were under the command of the Count of Perche.

The royalists who occupied the Mountsorrel Castle were no match for the army of rebels and the French prince. They had to withdraw to Nottingham to avoid the blood-spill, and Mountsorrel was freed simply by a display of force. Somewhat disappointed in the lack of resistance, the barons and soldiers searched for an opportunity, which presented itself not long after. Fifty miles northeast of Mountsorrel Castle lie Lincoln, with a castle that had resisted the rebels throughout the Barons' War. Lincoln Castle was besieged for a very long time, and when the rebels heard of the barons' forces being so near, they begged for help. Fitzwalter and de Quincy were eager to help their fellow rebels while Louis stayed in London. However, Nottingham was on their way to Lincoln. To avoid the royalist forces stationed there, the barons decided to turn east and cut their path through the agricultural lands of the Vale of Belvoir, where they looted and pillaged as they went. Taking this route, the baronial forces managed to approach Lincoln unchallenged and without any losses.

William Marshal was at Northampton when the news of the barons' army joining the besiegers at Lincoln arrived. He took the opportunity of Louis' forces being divided and tried to destroy them. He rode for four days from Northampton to Newark, but instead of going straight to Lincoln, he made a detour to the west, positioning himself to approach Lincoln from the northwest. If the rebels expected any help to come to the Lincoln royalists, they expected it to come from the southwest. He didn't just have the advantage of surprise on the battlefield; he also had access to the castle's west entrance, as it was not yet controlled by the rebels. The rebels didn't know about the existence of the small western gate. It was discovered by Peter de Roches, Bishop of Winchester, who rode with William Marshal. Marshal took the opportunity of a circuitous approach to Lincoln to bring news to the royalists that help was on its way.

The royalist army was accompanied by the legate Guala, who was prepared to excommunicate the French troops and absolve the English. Marshal addressed his troops, promising them honor and lifting their spirits. He was so eager to head to battle, his biographer notes, that he rode without his helmet and was called back to be properly armed. Marshal's bravery was also noted, as he was now over seventy years old. He used his massive size and his riding skills to thrust himself into combat.

The French and the barons had the advantage in numbers as they had twice as many knights. However, they were surprised by the determination of the loyalists as well as the presence of William Marshal. They were also pressed in between the castle walls they besieged and the cathedral that was behind them. General confusion and panic took over the rebel forces. Part of Louis' forces accompanied the barons with Count Perche as their commander. The count was killed by William Marshal, and the French troops decided to fall back after the loss of their commander. They eventually rallied and tried to rejoin the rebel forces, but they were now caught between Marshal and the main body of the royalist army. Over four hundred knights were taken as prisoners that day. Among them were the barons Fitzwalter and de Quincy.

Louis was now forced to negotiate with the royalists, as he alone stayed behind in London and was spared from the agony of the battle at Lincoln. Guala wished to severely punish Louis' ecclesiastical supporter Simon Langton, while Louis tried to protect him. The negotiations failed, and the French summoned reinforcements. It was Blanche of Castile, the granddaughter of Henry II and Louis' wife, who took it upon herself to gather the fleet and send it over the English Channel to help her husband. However, William Marshal sent Hubert de Burgh, Henry's justiciar, who intercepted the fleet off the coast of Sandwich and executed its captain as a common pirate. He then took the French reinforcements as prisoners. Louis was now forced to accept the terms offered to him during the negotiations. He renounced the throne and made an oath never to help the English rebels again. He did not leave England empty-handed, however. He was given an indemnity of 10,000 marks (almost £7,000 sterling) which was paid over a year. Louis also had to promise he would convince his father Philip, King of France, to return Henry's lands in France. Upon his arrival in France, Louis joined the Albigensian Crusade in the south of France. The barons were not severely punished either, and it was William Marshal who made sure the punishment was not too onerous. They were given amnesty, as well as freedom from all possible ransoms, and their lands were restored. Only the clergy who supported the rebellion didn't get back their lands, and that was considered punishment enough.

Later, reflecting on the events of First Barons' War, Henry III accused Marshal of betraying him by not punishing the barons and by not finishing off Louis. But Marshal stuck to his principles. He fought the war as a perfectly chivalrous knight, not as a bearer of royalist ideology. The rebelling barons were already excommunicated, and Marshal saw no reason to proclaim them traitors. Some historians see Marshal's decision not to punish the barons as a wise move. It helped heal the wounds England was left with due to the civil war. The power of the twenty-five was destroyed, as Fitzwalter and Quincy were beaten by the best knight in England, William Marshal. Even though the barons lost their power, the central ideas of the Magna Carta continued to live on through the reissued Great Charter of 1216.

Chapter 7 – Henry III and the Magna Carta

Despite winning the First Barons' War, William Marshal faced great trouble while trying to restore royal authority throughout the country. Part of his inability lay in the fact that the barons who remained loyal to the Crown now asked for a reward after the civil war. William was unable to give them lands, as was the custom, because he had given them back to rebelling barons. Consequently, the Loyalists started showing less interest in the politics of the Crown, if not openly abandoning them. Furthermore, William tried to restore the Crown's right to approve marriages and wardships, but he failed. Where he was successful was in restoring the royal bench of judges and reopening the royal exchequer.

Henry's government issued the Charter of the Forest in 1217, which played a role in giving back the governance of the forests to the Crown. To the Normans who had ruled England since William the Conqueror, the forest was an enclosed area in which the king (and sometimes other aristocrats) had the exclusive right to hunt, cut wood, or use the grasslands, heathland or wetlands that were included in the common term "forest." Kings Richard and John started including more and more areas of England in the royal forest, expelling people who inhabited the areas or simply forbidding them to live off the land. At its widest, one-third of the land of southern England was assumed to be the royal forest. Common people were forced to leave or die of starvation as they had no right to cultivate the lands or use it in any other way to sustain themselves.

The Charter of the Forest was issued together with the reissued Magna Carta as its complementary charter. Later it would be joined to the Magna Carta, but for now, it was a separate document that provided a certain degree of freedom and protection for the people who used the forest areas, mainly for their animals to graze or to grow their food. The first clause of the Forest Charter offered protection for all those who used the forest land as pastures for their animals and were already the inhabitants of the land. The ninth clause allowed all those who did not live in the areas of the forest to bring their livestock to graze in exchange for money. The Forest Charter also allowed people who lived in the forest area to build mills, fish preservation facilities, marl-pits, ditches, or gardens. The only condition was not to injure any neighboring lands. Clause ten banned the death penalty and mutilation as punishments for those who hunted in the forest. However, they still had to pay fines or face imprisonment.

By the times of the Tudors, the Forest Charter was mainly used to protect the timber industry and keep it in royal hands. Some clauses of this charter were enforced until 1970 through special courts that dealt with those who broke the law. The Forest Charter is the longest remaining medieval statute, as it was valid from 1217 until 1971. Finally, it was replaced with the still-active Wild Creatures and Forest Laws Act of 1971, which abolished the royal right to wild animals.

William Marshal fell ill in 1219 and believed he was dying. To prepare the new regency, he summoned the barons, Henry III, the papal legate Pandulf Verraccio, the royal justiciar Hubert de Burgh, and Peter des Roches, Bishop of Winchester. It was the Bishop who claimed the right of regency, but William refused him by appointing the papal legate, Verraccio. He had no trust in any of the aristocracy or clergy he summoned. William was invested into the order of the Knights Templar while on his deathbed due to his service in the crusade. He died on May 14, 1219, and was buried in the Temple Church in the London headquarters of the Templar Knights. His tomb can still be seen there and is open to visitors.

Pandulf Veraccio organized a new government around three ministers: himself, Peter de Roches, and Hubert de Burgh. They were appointed at Oxford by a great council of nobles. The new government had little success, as their authority was mainly dependent on this council of nobility. The bad luck of Henry III's government ended in 1220 when Pope Honorius III allowed Henry to be crowned for the second time. This act of renewed coronation had the purpose of strengthening the authority of the king. Barons, under the threat of excommunication, swore a new oath to Henry, promising they would repay their debts and give back the royal castles.

Meanwhile, Stephen Langton received the approval to return to England in 1219. However, it was not until 1221 that he regained the title of Archbishop of Canterbury. Langton returned to the political scene of England and took his seat at the triumvirate of councilors who guarded an under-aged king. It was two years later, in 1223 when King Henry III was finally proclaimed to be of the age to rule on his own. In January 1224, at Westminster Abbey, a council was held with Langton acting as spokesman for the barons. They called for the confirmation of the reissued Magna Carta, as it had already been sealed by the papal legate and the late regent, William Marshal. They were uncertain whether the king would ever acknowledge the Great Charter with his seals, and they insisted on reminding him.

Royal councilor William Brewer fought vigorously against the Magna Carta, claiming the liberties the barons demanded were extorted by force and therefore not valid. It was king Henry III who intervened to calm the situation that yet again threatened to divide his kingdom. He swore he would abide by the Great Charter, but he failed to give it a formal confirmation with royal seals.

In France, Louis VIII was now king, and he took advantage of Henry's weak government while he was still considered a minor by forcefully taking the remaining English lands on the continent, namely the provinces of Poitou and Gascony. To regain his territories, Henry needed money, and the royal council at Westminster approved a tax of £40,000 for the army. The barons issued a condition for Henry. They demanded he reissue the Magna Carta and the Charter of the Forest in exchange for their help. The king declared that the charters were given to the people with his free will and finally confirmed them with his royal seal on February 11th, 1225. The content of the reissued Great Charter was similar to that of the 1216 version, with some crucial differences.

In new words, the Magna Carta now gave the impression that it was solely the king's idea to reissue the Great Charter. This was a huge difference from the Charters of 1215 and 1216, which state the king approved of them by the advice of his councilors. In the 1225 version, there is no list of advisors or councilors that helped with the Magna Carta. There is only the king's name and those of the witnesses to the Charter. Among the mentioned witnesses are three loyalists who advised King John at Runnymede: the Earl of Salisbury, the Earl of Warenne, and Hubert de Burgh. Also, six of the barons who opposed John in the civil war were listed on the reissued Charter: Robert Fitzwalter, Gilbert de Clare, Hugh Bigod, Robert de Ros, Richard de

Montfichet, and William d'Aubigny. William Brewer, a councilor who had opposed the Charter back in 1223, was now listed as a witness who endorsed the reissued version.

A new, final clause was added to the Magna Carta to explain the reason behind the reissuing.

"And for this our grant and gift of these liberties ... the archbishops, bishops, abbots, priors, earls, barons, knights, freeholders, and all of our realm have given us a fifteenth part of all their movables."[15]

After the Magna Carta was reissued, Stephen Langton threatened excommunication for anyone who violated it. Two years later, Langton managed to gain permission for his exiled brother Simon to come back to England. Having Simon—a very passionate supporter of the baronial movement back in 1215—to fight by his side, Stephen gained formal confirmation of the Great Charter by Pope Gregory IX in January 1228. The pope's admission of the Charter was very important for its sustainability, as he was still supreme pontiff and feudal overlord of England.

Langton died in July 1228. He was eighty years old but still had a very clear mind before his death. A man without whom the Magna Carta would never have existed, Langton was a great scholar and a reformer of the English church. History knows him for many deeds, such as opening the council at Osney, whose decrees from 1222 are known as the earliest provincial canons. But it was his achievement to bind the Magna Carta and the church together that is still regarded as his greatest feat.

When Henry III took the rule of his kingdom in his own hands, he realized the relationship of the Crown with the barons was not being repaired. He and the barons quarreled over the same issues they had during his father's reign. Henry showed the same unrealistic desire to regain his dynastic lands in France as his father had. He favored foreigners who inhabited his court, and many native nobles felt undesired and believed they did not have the protection of the law.

---

[15] Magna Carta Translation, Final Clause. (n.d.). Retrieved from https://www.archives.gov/exhibits/featured-documents/magna-carta/translation.html

The barons' role in the government started decreasing compared to their role during Henry's minority. Furthermore, Henry had the habit of bypassing the offices of the state that were run by domestic nobles, whose role was to limit the king's control over the kingdom. He relied on a home office, an administration that ran his household. While he continued to summon the royal council and Parliament during the 1230s, he preferred the advice of intimate friends from the court.

During the middle years of his reign, Henry III faced yet another barons' rebellion, which seemed to be a continuation of the civil war his father fought against. The barons wanted to revive the panel of twenty-five or organize a similar committee that would have a direct check on the king. They drew inspiration from the Magna Carta itself, and even though they failed at defending the liberties the Great Charter gave them, they managed to draw the public eye to it.

Once Henry III came of age and started ruling England on his own, his personality changed. He was often described as too pious, lazy, and overly trusting of his household. His views were often shaped by his advisors, and he was generally regarded as a naïve ruler. He was not able to exercise his own judgment on the propositions he was offered by his closest friends. He modeled his rule after King Edward the Confessor, who was proclaimed a saint but was hardly engaged in the rule of his own country. Henry compared his authority over England to the pope's authority over the church, relying too much on religious views and the sacramental characteristics of kings.

Because of this regard of kingship, Henry tried to evade the restrictions the Magna Carta imposed on him. He could not annul it, as it was the document that kept the barons satisfied, at least to some extent. Instead, he took it upon himself to appoint officials and patronage and make political decisions, as the Magna Carta did not give specific details on how the barons should be involved in such things. The barons felt excluded from the political world of their very own country, and they believed that Henry was acting against the Magna Carta. The reissued Magna Carta of 1225 was stripped of the security clause of John's Charter, and the barons and bishops were forced to search for other ways to enforce the Magna Carta on the king. Henry wasn't concerned about the threats of excommunication that followed breaking the promises of the Magna Carta. He had the protection of the pope in Rome.

Henry III came into conflict with his justiciar, Hubert de Burgh, whose office in Westminster fought for the control of the government. In 1232, Henry removed Hubert from the office and had him arrested and his lands confiscated. Peter des Roches, the bishop of Winchester who was a passionate advocate for the authoritarian administration of John's rule, became the king's favorite advisor. It was des Roches who urged Henry to recover the lost French lands of his dynasty, but the endeavors in Poitou failed (1230-1242). Although he did regain Gascony, Henry lost other oversea territories that had been under English rule until then.

Henry III brought the foreign mercenaries he'd hired back to England and would not send them home. He continued to pay them, and he gave lands and castles to foreign nobles who enjoyed privileges in his court. To grant the lands to foreign magnates, Henry first had to take them away from domestic nobles, who were also des Roches' political opponents, and by doing so, he undermined the basis of landholding laws. It was this behavior that started a great crisis in 1232. Eventually, this crisis would result in another reaffirmation of the Magna Carta.

The first to complain about the king's new policies was Richard Marshal, son of William Marshal and the 3rd Earl of Pembroke. A new civil war broke out with Peter des Roches on one side and Richard Marshal and his followers on the other. During this revolt, Henry III was unable to gain military advantage over the united rebels, and he started to fear that Louis of France would come back to England and take advantage of the unrest in England to seize even more territories for France. The Archbishop of Canterbury summoned several great councils during 1234, in which he tried to persuade Henry to dismiss des Roches. Finally, des Roches was disgraced, and Henry agreed to peace.

Henry III did learn a lesson or two from the crisis that shook England from 1232 to 1234. He was reminded that the Magna Carta had the power to place him under the law and that earls, barons, and bishops were willing to judge him. Hubert de Burgh was restored as justiciar, and the king had to return the lands to the nobles who were injured during de Roches' service as the king's advisor.

It seems that King Henry III did not learn his lessons from this crisis until the end. The barons were right to be afraid of the king's subsequent behavior. Henry continued to interfere in lawsuits against tenants, even though the Magna Carta guaranteed them the liberties of their courts. After 1234, there was a lack of general justice in the kingdom, as Henry denied or delayed the prosecution of his close royal officials. Again, among those who enjoyed the king's protection were his foreign friends of the court—for example, the uncles to his wife, Eleanor of Provence, or his Lusignan half-brothers who were seeking their fortune in England. Once more, the native barons were left aside, feeling unwelcome at the royal court and outside of the law. Henry also allowed corruption to grow among the judges of his court, as he would often turn a blind eye toward the crimes his family and friends committed.

In the countryside, however, Henry III could not impose order, and local leaders rose to power. The barons were left to deal with the peacekeeping of their counties as the royal sheriff network collapsed. Domestic nobles lost all respect they had for their king, especially after he proved to be an incompetent military commander by losing all French territories by 1253. Throughout his military campaigns, Henry was always in need of money but was unable to persuade the barons to consent to money-grants due to a lack of capable advisors. The only thing he was capable of doing was raising taxes, as advised by his foreign friends. He exploited the Jews with heavy tallages, or land taxes, which resulted in the destruction of the Jewish community in medieval England. He also indulged in repossessing alienated royal lands to finance his war. He exploited the royal forest, which was protected by the Forest Charter. Instead of gathering enough money to finance his army in France, Henry III only managed to agitate his subjects, who saw his behavior as yet another violation of the Magna Carta. The barons insisted that Henry should reaffirm the Magna Carta in 1253, and in return, they promised financial aid for his campaign in Gascony. But it proved that this time, reaffirmation wasn't enough, as Henry continued abusing his rule.

Due to Henry's inept rule, a new crisis arose in the 1250s that inspired a new major reform movement among the nobles and clergy. The two groups were pulled together, as piety penetrated noble society. The clergy had a huge role in focusing the attention of the new rebellion to the Magna Carta. In 1258, the Archbishop of Canterbury openly accused Henry of violation of the churches' liberties, and those granted by the Magna Carta. Specifically, they claimed Henry kept ecclesiastical positions open so that he could enjoy the income they were bringing, as the king took it upon himself to appoint church officials. They continued pointing out how this behavior violated the Magna Carta on three occasions. The church also wanted to be involved in episcopal elections, as they saw elections as their domain. The Great Charter of King John granted the freedom of election to the church, a point which even Pope Innocent III embraced.

On the other hand, the barons were offended by how Henry III dealt with the distribution of patronage. They saw the king granting lands and castles to foreigners instead of domestic nobles. Even royal officials were alarmed when the king started granting large portions of land that were bringing income to the Crown to his half-brothers and his wife's uncles, the foreigners. This resulted in the dissipation of the Crown's resources, and the royal administrators could not ignore it. There were even suspicions of a secret government that ruled from within the royal household since the justiciar position had remained vacant since 1232. Also, the royal chancellor was no longer in charge of the royal seal since, in 1238, Henry took the responsibility on himself. Once more, the failings of the king cried for the reaffirmation of the Magna Carta, but it wouldn't be enough. The barons were left powerless, and they did not influence the king's choice to appoint royal officials.

It was the "Sicilian Business" that proved Henry III had a bad habit of listening to the flawed council of his foreign relatives and friends. In 1254, Henry accepted the offer from the pope to take over Sicily and gift its throne to his second son, Edward. Pope Innocent IV was in a personal vendetta war with the Hohenstaufen family, which had imperial authority over Italy. To speed up the arrival of Henry's army in Sicily, the Pope offered Henry a large sum of money, which he invested in the campaign. But soon after, Innocent was succeeded with Alexander IV, who refused to pay for Henry's campaign. Instead, he demanded Henry return the money he was given by Innocent. The sum was enormous, totaling £90,000, and Henry was unable to pay it. He turned to Parliament, asking for the barons' help, but they refused him. He attempted to gain Parliament's assistance for three more years, but Alexander was unhappy with the delay, so he sent an envoy to England threatening to excommunicate the king if he couldn't pay his debts to Rome. Parliament yet again refused to help Henry, who started extorting the money out of the senior clergy. He made them sign blank charters, which he then used as a promise that they would assist the king in raising the money for the efforts in Italy. In this way, he gathered around £40,000. The war in Italy had no support from his nobles and thus culminated in open revolt in 1258.

Chapter 8 –Second Barons' War and Edward I

The revolt started when seven barons formed an alliance with the goal of expelling King Henry III's half-brothers, the Lusignans, out of England. Among them was even a foreigner, Simon de Montfort, Earl of Leicester, who was French by origin. He married the king's sister and gained titles, but soon after, he fell out of the king's grace. His motivation for joining the revolt might have been personal, but he became the loudest advocate of reforms that would be beneficial not only to the barons but also to the knight class. Knights were also suffering as the government isolated the king, who allowed profit and financial advantages only to the people closest to him. Other barons who forged the alliance with them were Roger and Hugh Bigod, John Fitzgeoffrey, Peter de Montfort, Peter de Savoy, and Richard de Clare. These seven barons also gained the support of Queen Eleanor, who saw benefits in expelling the Lusignans out of the kingdom.

The baron's revolt of 1258 is considered the second great crisis in the rule of Henry III. They sought, once more, to restrain the king's authority, and they wished to move beyond the Magna Carta and secure permanent baronial involvement in the government, to control the king and put him under the rule of law. They also wished to reform the state offices so that they would start serving the kingdom, not just the king. The barons started the revolt slowly by showing up at Parliament sessions often to voice their demands and express their views of the kingship. After a relatively short time, the seven barons started demanding the changes with aggression, and Henry could no longer deny the danger of a new civil war. However, the barons faced a dilemma. There was nothing in their power to make the king accept the reforms if they wished to avoid violence, which could mark them as oath breakers and have them arrested for treason. They decided to treat the king as a mentally ill, incompetent ruler whose advisors needed to be changed. They sought to return the body of the councilors as the king's guardians, just as in the years of his minority. The barons formed "*le commun de Engleterre,*" or, as translated in modern English, "the community of the realm," a society that had the power to speak for the whole kingdom.

In June 1258, during the parliament session in Oxford, a demand was presented that the king should be faithful to the oath he made while reissuing the Magna Carta in 1225. Parliament proceeded with the insistence that both the king and the "community of the realm" should form a committee that would reform the government. Each party had to nominate twelve representatives, who would become the members of the committee and would work together to construct the acceptable reforms. This committee started their work and issued a series of governmental experiments that would last until 1265. They concentrated on searching for a way to limit the king's power and broadened the responsibilities of the English government. The measures passed by this parliament meeting are known as the Provisions of Oxford.

The committee came up with the idea of two councils that would share the power with the king. One would consist of fifteen officials chosen in equal numbers by the king and by the barons. The other council would be made of twelve who would be appointed by the barons alone. Their role would be to deal with the common laws and the business of the kingdom and the king. The barons wanted the full restoration of the justiciary and chancellor's offices, but they also demanded that these offices be separated from the king's household. The next to undergo reform would have been the office of the exchequer, which would prevent the king from shifting the financial flow toward his household. However, the implementation of such a reform would take away the king's executive power and reduce him to a puppet monarch.

In the protests of Henry's rule, the Magna Carta was often cited, mostly by the clergy, who shaped the revolt into a moral crusade. They also shamed the nobles into joining them by calling them "modern princes who oppress poor folk."[16]. Minor nobles, knights, and freeholders joined the barons and urged for reforms in local governments. The desire for change spread throughout the whole kingdom, including the countryside. In October 1259, the knights were granted the Provisions of Westminster, which reaffirmed the Magna Carta and the Forest Charter. It limited the office of the sheriff

---

[16] Carpenter (1999), 339; Maddicot (1994), 353-5.

to native knights who were to be elected annually and who would receive a salary for the job. The Provisions also restricted the authority of magnates in their courts, granting liberties to all free men who were the subjects of their jurisdictions. This clause always existed in the Magna Carta, but it was never implemented until 1259 when the council of twelve heard the complaints of the common people.

Cooperation between the king and the council was impossible, and the new constitution lasted for only two years. It collapsed in April 1261, when Henry III wrote to the pope asking for absolution from the oaths with which he supported the decisions of Parliament. To appease the people, the king tried to reassure them that he would still respect the charters, both the Magna Carta and the Charter of the Forest. However, Henry started replacing sheriffs who were elected by the barons, and he took control over some of the royal castles. The barons, with Simon de Montfort as their leader, once more united and started a government that would operate independently of the king. This time, they did not have the support of the queen, who helped her husband raise a mercenary army. Threatened by civil war, the barons were forced to back down. Simon was exiled to France, and the resistance of the barons was over, for the moment. Henry continued abusing his power by bullying his political opposition and extorting money from the Jews with high taxes. He continued to enjoy his authority over the kingdom until 1263, when the pope decided to reverse his judgment of the Oxford and Westminster Provisions, confirming their legitimacy. The country easily slipped back into civil war, as the barons believed they had the support of Rome.

Simon de Montfort was now able to return to England and gather the rebelling barons around him. The civil war broke out in October of 1263 between King Henry III, who had the support of his son Edward, and the loyalist barons and de Montfort, backed by the radically-oriented nobility. The rebels persuaded knights to join their cause, and together they started disposing of the evidence of their debts to the Jews to avoid paying them. As the Jews were considered the property of the Crown, the returned loans would end up in the king's hands. Five hundred Jews died when London rose in revolt. The rebels managed to completely replace the royal household of intimate friends of the king who acted as his councilors.

The war dragged on, and Montfort's victory at the Battle of Lewes in 1264 seemed to be the decisive battle. Montfort took complete control over the government, but he could not get rid of the king, as he was an anointed monarch. His authority had no legitimacy. The only path Simon de Montfort could take was to rule in the name of King Henry III, whom he held captive. To broaden his support, he ordered four knights from each county to come to the parliament sessions. He did not include only the knights in Parliament; he also invited merchants, thus widening the definition of the community in the kingdom.

Simon did not rule for long since some barons saw him as an obstacle to making peace with the king. He could not keep his followers united, and soon, some defected. Only a year after the Battle of Lewes, the royalist army defeated the reformist barons at Evesham, and it took only a few days for Henry III to nullify all the reforms implemented by Montfort. Simon Montfort was killed during the battle, and the barons no longer had anyone to unify them behind their cause.

The Second Barons' War failed to restrict the king's power. However, the Magna Carta was still at the very center of English law and politics. The king issued the Dictum of Kenilworth in 1266, with which he pronounced the reconciliation of the rebels. Once again, Henry III made a promise that he would abide by the Magna Carta and the Forest Charter. The king's heir, Lord Edward, became the de facto ruler alongside his father. He had sympathy for some of the reforms executed in 1259, and he secured the enactment of these reforms with the Statute of Marlborough. The Magna Carta was included in this statute, as Edward confirmed that all articles of the Great Charter would be respected equally, whether they concerned the king or the people.

However, once he became the sole king of the realm, Edward I governed England in the same manner as his father and grandfather. He strictly followed the Angevin tradition of preserving and expanding royal power. However, unlike his predecessors, Edward succeeded in bolstering the Crown's position as he enjoyed his rights to the fullest extent. One major difference between Henry III and Edward was that the later came to the throne as an adult, already having vast experience in how to govern. He was more capable of maintaining an efficient administration even through warfare, which was characteristic of his rule. He was determined to defend Gascony, the last English possession in France. He also tried to extend the English kingdom by taking over the whole British island. Of course, all this warfare demanded revenue-raising measures, which again oppressed and angered his subjects. In the last decade of his rule, a resistance formed once again and asked for the confirmation of the charters.

Edward I was, for a long time, considered an image of a strong and righteous monarch and the ideal image of a ruler, as he was a warrior-king who transformed the English administration and common law and was also known for his Christian piety and chivalry. However, modern historians believe that if he had ruled for just a bit longer, Edward would've turned England into an absolute monarchy, such as France was. As it stands, Edward is considered one of the fathers of the English Parliament, which finally settled on having regular sessions. Edward's parliament saw fit to replace the baronial committees with knights and townspeople who acted as spokesmen of their social classes. But this parliament also served as a body that allowed the king to legally raise taxes whenever he wished. The wars Edward was so eager to fight cost a lot more than a 13th-century king could afford.

The first time Edward confirmed the Magna Carta and the Forest Charter was in 1276, which resulted in a lack of any kind of political crisis that would disturb the early years of his reign. This period is often highlighted by historians as the high point of Medieval England.

In the second part of his rule, in his mature years, Edward's government violated the spirit of the Magna Carta. His problems were always financial, as he often fought wars on multiple fronts, engaging himself against France, the Scots, and the Welsh. During the 1290s, it seemed as if there were no end to Edward's military campaigns, and he imposed heavy taxation on the kingdom to keep financing his armies. A once-popular king was now resented by his own people. A political crisis erupted in 1297 when the barons, clergy, bishops, and merchants formed an opposition. Once again, the Magna Carta had the spotlight in the political turmoil of England. Parliament used the Magna Carta as a weapon, demanding that it be confirmed and reworked, as some of the clauses required clarification. They asked for supplementary clauses which would impose the rule of law on the king in hopes it would end his constant demand for higher taxes.

During the 13ᵗʰ century, the Great Charter—the Magna Carta—was a widely known document, as every lawyer or landholder had a copy of it and used it as a legal handbook. All the classes who owned some property were especially attracted to the Magna Carta. They could grasp its significance, as it had clauses that defended their rights and liberties. The ecclesiastic order valued the Great Charter because it guaranteed the church's freedom, and it is no wonder that the clergy were the first to oppose Edward's abuse of power.

Edward I used church funds (around half of its income) to reward his royal clerks, and this was the reason for the quarrel between the king and the Archbishop of Canterbury, who wanted to reform the church. The Archbishop organized the reading of the Magna Carta during the ecclesiastic council, after which he threatened excommunication for anyone who violated the freedom of the English church. He also ensured that all people could have access to the Great Charter and ordered its display in all cathedrals and churches. On Edward's orders, these copies of the Magna Carta were taken down as a clear sign of his resentment toward the Archbishop's decisions. The English clergy appealed to Pope Boniface VIII, who was eager to show his dominance over Edward, who ruled as a secular monarch. In 1296, the pope issued a bull that forbade the king from taxing the church and the clergy without the permission of the pontiff. The English clergy hoped for a different outcome, as this papal bull threw them into a dilemma. They were now either to disobey their secular ruler—the king—or the pope himself. They chose to disobey Edward, who used the opportunity to place them outside of royal protection. This meant they were now outlaws. In the end, the pope agreed to a compromise in 1297 that allowed rulers to tax the clergy without papal permission but only in times of emergency. However, the pop never defined what would be considered an emergency, so the monarchs were free to come to their own conclusions.

Edward I did not fail to anger the merchants either. He raised the customs taxes, which remained known as *maltote*, or evil toll, as named by the people of that time. In July of 1294, the king ordered an increase of the tax on all moveable wealth. He also made merchants sell wool to him, and then the Crown would resell it for a much higher profit used to fund the war. He also angered the barons by ordering them to fight in Flanders, where the barons had no interests of their own and their ancestors had never set foot before, a land to which they had no ties or any reason to fight for.

The resentment of the opposition was so great that Edward took care to reinforce the royal castles in case the civil war broke out while he was on his campaign in Flanders. Dissatisfaction with how high the tolls were resulted in two earls bringing their armies to the exchequer, forbidding the office to collect taxes. Edward I left his son and heir, Edward Caernarvon, to deal with the crisis that rose in England. In October 1297, he summoned Parliament, promising the confirmation of the Magna Carta and the Forest Charter. However, the barons insisted on adding new clauses to the Magna Carta that would limit the king's power, and Edward had to refuse them. Instead, the clauses were published in a separate document that contained six promises known as the Confirmation of the Charters. The first clause made Edward promise to keep the Magna Carta and the Forest Charter, as confirmed by his father, Henry III. Another clause said that the charters needed to be sent to all cathedrals, where they would be read to the people twice a year. Three years later, in 1300, as the war with the Scots raged on and Edward tried to raise taxes once more, the bishops had the Magna Carta confirmed once again. This confirmation of the Charter is important in history because it was the first time it was read to people in the English language.

Edward I did manage to free himself of the confirmation of the Magna Carta of 1300 by making a deal with the merchants, who agreed on increased customs in 1303. An agreement made with only one group instead of the whole community during a parliament session violated the spirit of the Magna Carta. However, the king went even further and made a deal with the pope. He was granted absolution from the promises presented in the Confirmation of the Charters in exchange for consent to the pope's levy of a tax on the English church. Even though the king disavowed the Confirmation of the Magna Carta, it remained in the memory of his subjects, and they pressed hard on their monarch for new confirmations.

The legal profession started emerging in the 14th century, and it gave the Magna Carta a pivotal place in English law. Lawyers of the late medieval age, who practiced outside of universities, resented canon and Roman law and instead glorified the Magna Carta since it was the native English law.

Chapter 9 - The Late Medieval Period and the Tudors

Henry VII, Founder of the Tudor Dynasty

(Source:
https://en.wikipedia.org/wiki/House_of_Tudor#/media/File:Enrique_VII_de_Inglat
erra,_por_un_artista_an%C3%B3nimo.jpg)

The Magna Carta continued to be confirmed throughout the 13th and 14th centuries, but later it was shadowed by high politics and remained in the background until the 17th century. The rapid economic changes and endemic lawlessness that marked the period had a higher priority for the barons than the Magna Carta. However, the Magna Carta wasn't entirely forgotten. It was confirmed eight times during the 15th century, which is, nevertheless, significantly lower than the thirty confirmations it had received in the previous century. The Great Charter continued to be observed in parliamentary and judicial proceedings during the late Middle Ages. During the reign of Edward III (1327-77), six statutes were enacted, and they defined the Charter's promise of what was to become the "due process of law." The Magna Carta was used to teach the common law tradition of due process, not only to lawyers but also to the country's gentry. Legal expertise was essential for the landholding class, and it started to realize this.

Landholders considered the Magna Carta and the common law to be the best protectors of property rights.

The English Parliament had taken shape during the reign of Edward I, but it was in the times of Edward III that it went through key stages of development. When Parliament allowed spokesmen for the ranks bellow the barons and nobles, it became the protector of the liberties promised to the people by the Magna Carta. During the 14th century, each first petition of the parliament session was made by the House of Commons, which requested that the Great Charter and the Charter of the Forest be firmly followed.

The Magna Carta, the Forest Charter, and the Confirmation of the Charters of Edward I were considered sacred during the 14th century. Statutes that opposed this document were regarded as invalid. The practice continued during the reign of Edward III, who even called for the examination of the statutes to confirm they did not oppose the Magna Carta.

The reign of Edward II reversed the kingdom to the times of Henry III with the practice of a household government. Edward II was known for lavishing his friends with gifts in the form of money and lands with no regard for how useful these people were to the politics of the kingdom. Once more, the barons gathered to devise a plan on how to supervise the government. Personal rivalries obscured the importance of the Magna Carta and constitutional principles. Both factions, royalists and reformists, were prepared to take up arms and fight for control over the king and the government. Armed conflict erupted when the king refused to exile his closest friend Piers Gaveston, the first Earl of Cornwall, who had an enormous influence on the politics of England. In fact, contemporary chroniclers have said that, at the time, England was ruled by two kings, Edward II and Gaveston—one by name and the other by actions. It is said that Edward II preferred the company of his friend Gaveston to the company of his wife, Queen Isabella. It is no wonder she gave her support to the reformist barons. The king had to send his friend into exile in 1308, appointing him Lieutenant of Ireland. At the same time, he wrote to Pope Clement V, requesting that Gaveston be allowed to return to England. The Earl of Cornwall was permitted to return to England, but his relationship with the barons proved to be very difficult. Soon, his political enemies refused to be present in parliament meetings just because he was there. The barons petitioned King Edward to abandon Gaveston as his councilor and to instead admit the advisory body of twenty-one elected barons known as the Lords Ordainers, or simply Ordainers. Their goal was to carry out reform of both the government and the royal household. Edward accepted, and the Ordainers were elected from both the reformist faction and the royalists. They came up with a series of ordinances in 1311 for reordering the government. The Magna Carta had an important role in the construction of these ordinances. Articles 6 and 38 acknowledged that the monarch was bound by the Great Charter and that he would keep all points of the Magna Carta. The Charter was made as a standard for legislation in Article 31, which points out that if any statute conflicts with the Magna Carta or the Charter of the Forest, it is to be annulled.

Under the Ordinances of 1311, Edward was still the head of the government and chief of state, and he considered the Ordinances to be crippling to his royal executive power. When Gaveston was captured and killed by the barons, Edward was determined to gain release from the Ordinances. However, to secure a campaign in Scotland, he agreed to forgive the barons involved in Gaveston's death and to uphold the Ordinances. The king was quick to find a new favorite, Hugh Despenser the Younger, whose influence and acquisition of lands in Wales angered the barons once more. Edward II granted his army to Despenser in his land grab on the Welsh borders. The barons considered this move a direct violation of Clauses 29 and 39 of the Magna Carta, as the king was sending the army against his subjects. In 1321, Despenser's enemies occupied most of the parliament seats, and a vote to exile him and his father from England passed. The king tried to defend his favorite, calling on the Magna Carta because banishing Despenser "would be contrary to the common law of our realm."[17] At the Battle of Boroughbridge in 1322, the king's army defeated the baronial party, and the travesties of the trials similar to the one that exiled Despenser repeated. Twenty-five barons were executed, while others were either imprisoned or

[17] Thompson, Faith (1948), *Magna Carta: its role in the making of the English constitution, 1300–1629*, Minneapolis: University of Minnesota Press.,78.

fined for the roles they took against the king. The Magna Carta's guarantee that punishment must be a result of judgment was ignored, as trials by peers were not conducted. After these events, the Magna Carta grew in its importance once more.

The Parliament in York cited the Magna Carta's law of the land, and Despenser's exile was revoked. The Statute of York refused to acknowledge the Ordinances of 1311 and concluded that it was not the barons who knew what was best for the king and the kingdom. This revocation of the Ordinances did not influence the validity of the Great Charter, which continued to be reaffirmed when the occasion demanded it. Eventually, Edward II was forced to abdicate due to the political schemes of his own wife, Queen Isabelle of France, and her lover Roger Mortimer. The pair placed the king's underage son, Edward III, on the throne while they ruled as regents.

Once eighteen, Edward III took the kingdom into his own hands and banished his mother while executing Mortimer. His rule was one of warfare: he started the Hundred Years War (1338-1453) as he tried to recover the Plantagenet lands in France. The barons shared his enthusiasm for war, and as long as the king was giving royal privileges to the Parliament, the barons were happy to finance the war. They were also eager to recover the lands in France, which would bring them more prospects.

Edward III was succeeded by his grandson Richard II, whose rule was often described as weak, much like the rules of Henry III and Edward II, since they all held a household parliament filled with bad advisors. Like his two predecessors, Richard was forced to share executive power with the barons. He accepted the reform commission of 1386, known as the Lords Appellant, which resembled the Lords Ordainers of Edward II. At the time, the Hundred Years War was raging, but Richard was a king who sought peace. His barons were unsatisfied with his decision to pursue peace because they profited greatly from the war with France. In Richard II's later rule, it seems that the Magna Carta was forgotten. It continued to exist—it was never annulled, and lawyers continued to use it as a handbook for common law. But the citizens had lost their trust in common law, and while petitioning the king or Parliament, they never cited the Magna Carta. Even during the Peasants' Revolt in 1381, when the people made demands for their personal freedoms, they did not once call on the Magna Carta.

Richard II devoted himself to getting rid of Parliament's decision to share power with the Lords Appellant, and by 1388, he succeeded. After gaining all the executive power for himself, the king started a despotic rule. His enemies were either exiled or executed, and none of them were inspired by persecution to appeal to the Magna Carta's protection. Richard enforced his military tribunals, and the Court of the Constable and traditional common law courts were forgotten. During the totalitarian phase of his regime, King Richard II disinherited his own cousin, Henry Bolingbroke, who was exiled and whose lands and estates were confiscated. This action directly threatened the property rights of the aristocracy and pushed the magnates into rebellion. Richard was forced to face the rebels alone since he had no one's support. In 1399, Parliament started the process of disposition, forcing Richard to abdicate. Still, it was done in such a manner as to leave the impression that the king had abdicated of his own free will. Since Richard had no son, his closest relative who succeeded him was the same Henry Bolingbroke whom he had exiled. Bolingbroke was crowned Henry IV, first of the Lancastrian kings.

Periodic confirmation of the Magna Carta, which grew into a custom, ended during the reign of Henry VI, the last Lancastrian king. Historians explain that the importance of the Great Charter waned as England became a country of disorder and political disasters. But the Magna Carta was not forgotten. There is plenty of evidence that the Charter was cited and that defendants were appealing to its technical provisions. Also, lawyers and judges cited it for their occasional petty purposes. Appeals to the Charter's guarantee of due process are nonexistent during the times of the Lancastrian and Yorkist kings. The political scene where lawlessness ruled and the constant danger of coups d'état were fertile grounds for the kings' constant violations of Clauses 29 and 39. Amidst the changes that the 15th century brought, the Magna Carta was not in the center of political life anymore. Edward IV and Richard III, together with their Tudor successors, were often accused by their contemporaries of leading England to modern absolutism.

The councilor or prerogative courts of the Tudor times threatened the common law courts' existence. They were more efficient in enforcing law and order than the traditional common law courts were ever able to. Another downside of the common law courts was the corruption of the judges and the easy intimidation of the juries. With authoritarian procedures derived from Roman law, the tribunals were designed to bring swift justice, punish offenses that the common law prohibited, and strike awe and fear into the magnates.

Under the rule of the Tudors, the Magna Carta continued to be in the back of the political scene of England. Starting in 1399, the kingdom had a series of weak rulers, and the need for a strong government rose. Many people thought that sacrificing a few of their liberties was a small price to pay for a stable and orderly kingdom. With Henry VII and his successors came the Tudor despotism, and these rulers represent early examples of absolute monarchy, which was customary for 16th and 17th century Europe. However, today's historians believe that the Tudors could never exercise a truly despotic rule for the simple fact that they lacked resources. Besides lacking money, the Tudors had no standing army or a force that could police the country. They, too, depended on the support of the barons and state magnates to raise taxes. The Tudors were aware that the Crown had to keep the appearance of acknowledging due process, and in return, the judges and lawyers protected the Crown's privilege in the court.

When Henry VIII made the Anglican church independent from Rome, he violated the rights of his subjects. This only serves to show how little the Magna Carta was respected during his rule. He often imprisoned his political opponents without pressing any charges just to show his power over them. Only occasionally someone would call on the Magna Carta, claiming his rights and liberties as an Englishman. Even though the first clause of the Great Charter guaranteed the freedom of the English church, most of the Catholics who were persecuted by the king turned to the pope and his authority for arguments against royal supremacy. To understand why no aristocratic magnate rose in opposition to the rule of the Tudors, one must realize the atmosphere of their rule.

The English social and economic structure was no longer medieval, and the aristocracy lost their political influence. The rapid economic changes of the 16th century left the barons in confusion, and they were barely capable of adapting. Commerce replaced agriculture as a source of wealth, while inflation was rising and the expenses of a luxury life became unaffordable for many. The poverty the barons suddenly experienced drove them to flock around the king in hopes of earning his patronage. While the fortune of the aristocrats was falling, the gentry—the descendants of the medieval knights—were rising. Many of them won the election and became members of the House of Commons, and they finally started expressing their own political and religious concerns.

Another novelty of the 16th century was a cultural current from Italy known as humanism. The idea of a perfect gentleman who had the qualities of a medieval chivalric knight and knowledge of Greek and Roman philosophy occupied the minds of not only the aristocracy but also the gentry. Tudor subjects were living in a new age free from the chaos of civil war with a new, rejuvenated monarchy, enjoying the new teachings of humanism. Liberated from the papal grasp on their religion, the people of England saw no point in rebelling over the few liberties that were taken away from them.

With the invention of the printing press and the kingdom's thirst for knowledge, the Magna Carta returned to England's attention. Copies of it were printed as early as the 1480s, and together with other legal textbooks, the Great Charter was among the first books to be printed in the Kingdom of England. The first time the Magna Carta was published in full was in 1508 by an immigrant from Normandy, Richard Pynson, who became the "king's official printer." His prints of *Magna Carta, cum aliis antiquis statutis* became the most reprinted edition and the basis for the modern English translation.

Around the same time, due to humanism, an interest in England's history awoke. For the first time, people became aware of the controversy that followed King John and the signing of the Magna Carta. Until now, they had known the Great Charter only from the statute books and only its version from 1225. The 1215 version of the Charter became known through the work of Archbishop of Canterbury Matthew Parker, who gathered medieval manuscripts and held one of the most important collections, which he left to the University Library of Cambridge College. But the first printer to publish the translated version of the Magna Carta was George Ferrers, in 1579. Ferrers was a politician, poet, and a common lawyer who printed the full text of the Charter in English, not Latin. His translation is often clumsy, as he used more words than needed to describe certain terms. However, he did convey the general meaning of the document.

The recovery of the Magna Carta's version from 1215 shed new light on the dispute King John had with his barons, and the contemporary texts were often biased and openly supported the rebellion. However, the English public still avoided questions concerning the monarchy, English constitution, and English liberties. They were aware that the discussion of such issues was dangerous at a time when Tudors held England in their royal grip. There was no opposition strong enough to question the character of a Tudor's monarchy, no one brave enough to allow himself to be inspired by the Barons' Revolt and reclaim those liberties.

The meaning of the Magna Carta was, perhaps, most clearly grasped by the Puritans, who were under constant pressure for religious compliance under Elizabeth I. Some even argued that the first clause of the Magna Carta, which guaranteed the freedom of the "English Church," did not apply only to the Anglican church, but to all. The lawyers who took the cases of the Puritans resurrected the promises of the Great Charter, and pamphlets publicizing the liberties it guaranteed started circulating the country. Robert Beale and James Morice, both members of Parliament, composed treatises describing the Magna Carta as basic and unchangeable law—the law above all royal writs, the law of law. This upholding of the Magna Carta by the Puritans and their representatives prepared the way for the parliamentarians of the 17th century, who would use the Magna Carta against the Stuart monarchy that succeeded the Tudors.

Chapter 10 – The Revival of the Magna Carta

During the 17th century, the Magna Carta once more took a central place in the political and royal life of the English kingdom. The parliamentarians and common lawyers used the Great Charter to fight the royal prerogative reasserted by James I. During the 17th century in Europe, the trend was to support the divine right of the monarch. Considering modern European values, the Magna Carta was an anomaly, with its tradition of subjecting royal power to the rule of law. Queen Elizabeth I, the last ruler of the House of Tudor, was succeeded by James VI of Scotland, who upon being crowned, ruled as James I of England. Accustomed to the notion of a divine-right monarchy, he had little trouble adapting to Tudor authoritarianism. However, the combination of totalitarian notions in one monarch threatened Parliament's role in governing the kingdom. By the 1640s, the monarch's opponents faced the same problems as the barons of King John. They needed a solution for a king who refused to respect the law. As the problem was the same as in 1215, so was the answer: civil war. This time, instead of the barons, the leaders were parliamentarians, and the result of the 1642-48 civil war was far more eccentric. The king was executed, and England fell into a decade of experimental republican government.

The rule of the Stuart kings that led to the civil war during the reign of Charles I is comparable to the rule of King John, Henry III, and Edward I. James I issued a patent for monopoly over the trade of certain goods. He privileged his favorites, and the competition was often imprisoned for infringement. The victims understood such actions violated Clauses 29/39 of the Magna Carta. James canceled some of the monopolies to appease his opponents, but that wasn't enough. In 1624, Parliament issued a statute that limited royal monopolies. To raise revenues without Parliament's consent, the Stuart kings often turned to purveyance (the right of sovereigns to buy provisions at a fixed price that was much lower than the market value). Protests followed such actions, and the members of the House of Commons of the English Parliament cited the Magna Carta in their fight against the royals. However, the protests achieved nothing, as the

House of Lords did not want to provoke King James. Avoiding any conflict, Parliament decided to ignore the pleas of the Commons.

The Puritans continued their fight against the monarchs over the supervision of the church of England. Both Elizabeth I and her Stuart successors considered authority over the church to be their royal prerogative. However, Puritans, who were occupying more and more seats in the House of Commons, challenged this prerogative. They wanted total eradication of Papism and reconstruction of the Anglican church based on their own belief system. They named themselves Puritans as they sought to "purify" the church from the influence of Roman Catholic practices and finally turn it to clear Protestantism.

In the early 1620s, the members of the House of Commons demanded that their king, Charles I, reaffirm the Magna Carta. It was Sir Edward Coke—a lawyer, judge, and politician—who claimed that the Magna Carta was still valid when the king started to imprison those who refused to pay forced loans and taxes. Charles I was willing to confirm the Great Charter but refused to allow its reinterpretation. However, this did not please the Commons, who answered by issuing the Petition of Right, which asked for specific liberties for the English people, such as the restriction of taxation which did not gain Parliament's approval, forced billeting of soldiers, imprisonment without charge, and use of martial law. Clauses 29/39 of the Magna Carta took a central place in the Petition of Right. When it reached the House of Lords, some fully supported it, but others sought to change it and preserve some of the royal prerogatives. The Lords proposed a version of the petition that would be a compromise; however, the Commons, with Coke as their leader, strongly opposed it. When the petition reached Charles I, he had no choice but to accept it. Soon after, he broke his promises and started arresting members of the Commons without offering any reason. Many did not survive imprisonment and could not raise any objections. Charles I started his tyrannical rule, and Parliament did not assemble for the next eleven years, from 1629 until 1640.

Charles was convinced he could be a good ruler if he only wasn't constricted by Parliament, but he soon faced the problem of finding new revenue streams without Parliament's grants. To deal with this problem, Charles continued to break the promises of not only the

Magna Carta but also the Forest Charter by trying to extend the royal forests. He also exploited payments for coastal defense by extending its parameters to the whole kingdom, exclaiming that the entirety of England benefited from the royal navy. All these sources of revenue allowed him to collect enough money to enjoy times of peace. However, the king provoked a conflict in Scotland, and it was soon clear that the income was not enough. The king tried to force Anglican teachings on the Scottish church, which resulted in war in 1639/40. War debts forced the king to summon Parliament once more.

The first parliament session in 1640, known as the Short Parliament since it lasted for only three weeks, did not want to solve the king's financial issues until he granted his subjects assured liberties. The Magna Carta was once more at the center of attention, and the king could not gain control over Parliament. It had to be disbanded. The second parliament session, known as the Long Parliament, followed soon after and would exist until 1653 when Oliver Cromwell dissolved it. However, this Parliament had no more interest in solving the king's problems than the previous did.

It was this Parliament that sought to restrain the king's absolute power by trying to take control of the military from the king's hands. In 1641, there was a massive uprising in Ireland against the Protestants, and the king needed an army to deal with it. However, Parliament was reluctant, as they feared that Charles would use the same army against them. They issued a militia ordinance that represented a clear challenge to royal sovereignty and stated the king's responsibility to the kingdom's defense. In January 1642, the king issued an order for the imprisonment of five leaders of the radicals from the House of Commons. The five managed to escape, but a civil war broke out as a response to the king's attempt against Parliament.

The king was defeated. However, a second civil war broke out in 1648 between Parliament's Puritans and the radical Protestant soldiers. The Protestants were victorious, and they sent Charles I to trial in January 1649, when he was condemned and executed as a tyrant, traitor, and public enemy of the commonwealth. Before this event, the accusation of treason had been reserved for those who committed crimes against the Crown. But now, under a new military order with Oliver Cromwell at its head, treason was defined as the Crown's betrayal of the people.

The radical Protestants started their experiment with a republican regime in 1649, and it lasted until 1660, a period known as an interregnum. Soon, Cromwell faced the same problems as the king. He needed to gather money for the emergencies caused by civil war, but Parliament proved to be nothing more than a frustration. Oliver Cromwell started collecting taxes without the consent of Parliament, and he started arresting his opponents without showing due cause. When people appealed to the Magna Carta for protection, Cromwell ridiculed the document, often mocking it in crude language.

Two years after the death of Oliver Cromwell, in 1660, Charles II claimed the English throne. Even though royal rule was back, Charles couldn't simply refuse to accept all the constitutional changes that the Long Parliament had made during the civil war. He accepted the limitations placed on the king's power, but still, there was no clear definition of which domain of government belongs to the king and which to Parliament. The settlement that restored the king in England was a victory for the Magna Carta's principle of law limiting the king's power, although the victory was limited. The common law could only check the royal prerogative, not completely ban it.

The first parliament session after the crowning of Charles II in 1660 enacted legislation that ratified some of the principles of the Great Charter. General taxes now always needed parliament's approval but were also extended to other royal attempts to raise money, such as customs duties. Knights' fees and military tenures were abolished, leaving the king without his feudal sources of income. However, some royalists rose to complain about these yolks on the king's executive power, and the Commons answered by acting against the individuals who did not respect the Magna Carta. Judges, who stayed in the king's employment, often mocked the Magna Carta, stating that they were above it did not have to live by it. Such individuals were accused of endangering the people's liberties and had to make a public apology to Parliament.

The question of sovereignty remained unanswered during the rule of Charles II, mainly because he made certain it was never asked. He was unwilling to risk falling to the same fate as his father and, therefore, avoided provoking Parliament. Parliament stayed quiet, too, unwilling to press the king to solve the matter. In this way, both parties continued to work in a balance of powers, avoiding stirring the political scene of England, which had just ended its experimental phase as a republic.

It was during the rule of James II that the demand for resolving the sovereignty question arose. The brother and successor of Charles II, he incited a crisis in 1686 by reviving the Court of High Commission, a supreme ecclesiastic court in England established during the rule of Elizabeth I that had proclaimed Puritanism an offense. This court was dissolved in 1641 by the Long Parliament, and now, in James' vision, he had revived it. The Court of High Commission was no longer prosecuting Papists and Puritans; instead, it served as a means for Catholicism to infiltrate into the Anglican church. James manipulated various laws to appoint his Catholic co-religionists into government positions that were reserved only for those who belonged to the Anglican church. Royal propaganda used the Magna Carta, calling on the freedom of religion guaranteed by the Great Charter. The king's opponents were forced to fight against the freedom of religion as, by admitting it, they would confirm that it was in the king's domain to make and unmake laws.

When the royal son of James II was born, his opponents were angered that Catholic rule would continue, as they hoped the crown would pass to one of the king's daughters who were married to Protestant princes. To make sure no Catholic line would rule England, they invited James' eldest daughter Mary and her husband, William of Orange, head of the Dutch Republic, to come and take the crown as joint rulers. William accepted the invitation, accusing James of breaking the law and disrespecting the Magna Carta. William came to England in 1688 with an army to challenge James, but the king suddenly lost all his support and was forced to flee to France. The act of abandoning England was considered equal to abdication, and Parliament declared the post of monarch vacant. William and Mary were crowned as joint rulers, and the parliament assembly chose to ignore the old English customs of hereditary law that called for only male successors. By doing so, they changed the constitution and showed that the power they wielded was greater than the monarchs.

A new Magna Carta that would better define the rights of a king and the rights of his subjects was debated. The Bill of Rights was drafted and enacted in December 1689. The bill was a pragmatic document, as was the Magna Carta. It responded to the specific problems of James II's rule, listing twelve unlawful acts that James had committed followed by fifteen measures for correcting his wrongs. The king's right to issue decrees with the force of law was denied by this bill, and he was prohibited from gathering or levying taxes without Parliament's approval. It made it illegal for a king to have a standing army without the consent of Parliament, and the people were guaranteed their rights of jury trials. The coronation oath was reworded by another act to make sure the king would obey not only traditional law and customs but also the statutes of the Parliament— once more showing that the king would always be overpowered by Parliament if the need should arise. The possibility of an absolute monarchy in England died as Parliament made itself superior to the king. The Magna Carta continued to inspire Parliament, which issued writs and statutes that would grant more and more liberties to the people of England.

Chapter 11 – The New World and the Magna Carta

HUDSON BAY COMPANY

49°

N S

(e Mass)

PROVINCE OF QUEBEC

N H

N Y   MASS

R I

PA   N J   CONN

MD   DEL

VA

(Spain)

INDIAN RESERVE

N C

S C

GA

W FLA

E FLA

Proclamation Line of 1763

Boundary between Mississippi River and
49th parallel uncertain due to misconception that
source of Mississippi River lay further north

1775

The Thirteen Colonies (red)

(Source:
https://en.wikipedia.org/wiki/Thirteen_Colonies#/media/File:Map_of_territorial_gr
owth_1775.svg)

English common law and its liberties started spreading all over the globe during the expansion of the British Empire. However, the Magna Carta was not accepted everywhere equally. New territories brought new people to the British Empire, and those people had their own centuries-old laws and customs. The Magna Carta was purely a British heritage, and it continued to thrive only in colonies whose citizens were mostly British. The Great Charter continued to live in Canada, Australia, New Zealand, and the United States. However, nowhere did English common law influence the whole nation as much as in the first thirteen colonies in North America. There, the Magna Carta took on a new life and directly influenced the shaping of a new nation, The United States of America.

The settlers in North America were convinced they were still regarded as citizens of England. Bringing the Magna Carta with them, they thought it would give them protection from arbitrary government. They considered the Great Charter a contract between themselves and the king, and this contract spelled out all the obligations for both sides. In 1606, King James I even issued a charter that confirmed the rights and liberties of the Virginia Company. The charter stated that colonists would enjoy the same liberties and immunities as the people of England. Massachusetts got its own similar charter in 1629 that promised liberties to the colonists as if they were born within the Kingdom of England.

In 1765 and 1774, a reaffirmation of the charters was needed. The colonists were promised that they could keep all the freedoms their immigrant ancestors brought to America. The promise was made by both the Stamp Act Congress and the First Continental Congress. The liberties included not just freedom itself but also common law, by which they had the right of a trial by jury.

All the charters given to the colonies had a clause that was directly drawn from Clause 29/39 of the Magna Carta. The clause promises that no man's life would be taken, no man would be imprisoned, banished, or dismembered, and no man's lands would be taken or damaged unless the law was broken. Over the next century, all colonies would be given similar charters, with astonishingly similar clauses, and they all guaranteed the same rights directly taken from the Magna Carta.

Because of these charters given to the colonies in America, the English books of law were in high demand, especially the works of Edward Coke on the Magna Carta. Philadelphia published the 1225 version of the Magna Carta as part of William Penn's tract. William Penn was the founder of the Quaker colony, later known as Pennsylvania. In 1681, King Charles II granted Penn a charter with which he brought freedom of religion to his Quaker colony. In the colonies of North America, the law became the most popular profession since it promised not only profit but also status in society.

Many of the Founding Fathers of the United States were lawyers. Out of the fifty-six signed names on the Declaration of Independence, twenty-five belonged to lawyers. Among them, Thomas Jefferson is known for having the finest private library, with many English legal texts that offered their interpretations of the Magna Carta.

In the beginning, the colonies enjoyed privacy and were mostly left alone as the king and the English Parliament had little interest in them. For one hundred years, America was seen as nothing more than unprofitable new lands less valued than the sugar islands in the West Indies. But when the British Empire realized the American colonies' potential and tried to influence their economy, the people were already accustomed to their liberties. Suddenly, possession of America was regarded as the king's prerogative, and it was the king who decided to disallow the acts adopted by the colonial legislatures. Because the colonial legislatures had no clear relationship with the English Parliament, King George III dismissed their existence. It was the English Parliament that took upon itself the regulation of external trade. The members of Parliament started claiming that because possessions in America were gained either by conquest or by diplomatic measures with the native people, they did not fall under the jurisdiction of English common law. America was not a part of the motherland; therefore, America had no guarantee of enjoying the same rights and liberties. Soon, the English Parliament took authority over the colonies, claiming that they existed only to bring profit to the British Empire, and as such, must be taxed under separate economic policies. After the war with France (1755-1763), Parliament expected the American colonies to organize their own defenses and pay higher taxes, which now spread from trade to all aspects of life. The angered colonies were left with little choice but to fight to regain their freedoms. The Magna Carta was once more at the epicenter of the events, as the colonies often cited it in pamphlets and propaganda against the British Empire's government.

The first protests and uprisings started in 1765 when the English Parliament issued the Stamp Act, imposing more taxes on the colonists, especially for printed material. Newspapers, legal books, magazines, playing cards, and many other materials had to be printed on stamped paper produced in London. The stamp was a revenue stamp that had to be paid in British currency, not the colonists' paper money. The colonists implemented the slogan "no taxation without representation" in their fight to regain the liberty of no taxation without consent, which was guaranteed by the Magna Carta. Even John Adams, in his draft for the community protest, wrote that the stamp violated the British constitutional principle that no man would be taxed without his consent given in person or by a proxy. For him, the British government's actions directly conflicted with the Magna Carta. However, England did not react, and new taxes followed in 1767 and 1773 when the East India Company gained a monopoly on selling tea to the colonies. The colonists were outraged by these moves and decided not just to boycott the company's tea but to throw their ships' cargo into the sea in an event known as the Boston Tea Party. The protests that followed were violent, and Parliament was pushed into issuing the Intolerable Acts of 1744, by which they closed the Boston port and suspended the charter given to the Massachusetts colony in 1629. The goal was to punish Boston and set an example to other colonies of what would happen to them if they did not obey the English Parliament's authority.

The American armed rebellion that followed took as its precedent the uprising of the barons who had extorted the Magna Carta from King John. By the colonists' interpretation, the barons were heroes of popular liberty. The seal of Massachusetts was redesigned during these times to represent a militiaman with a sword in one hand and the Magna Carta in the other. In fact, the protesters combined their modern views of law and the traditional appeals of the Great Charter in their war against the Stamp Act. It was the natural law that pushed forward the political thought of the American revolutionaries. The Magna Carta was even cited in the Declaration of Independence, which was signed on July 4, 1776. The natural rights of life, liberty, and the pursuit of happiness found their place within the Declaration in the bold words of Thomas Jefferson. The Declaration continued with a statement that if the government threatens these natural rights, it is the people's right to alter or abolish said government. The Declaration continued by accusing the king of breaking the contract between himself and the colonists when he took away the charters granted to America. He was also accused of staging a war against his own people, who had left England as free men only to become slaves, losing their basic rights as citizens of the British Empire once they set foot in the colonies. King George III became the symbol of England's tyranny over its colonies, even though it was Parliament that came up with all the measures to profit from the Americas. This mistake wasn't unintentional. It was easier for people to grasp a fight against the monarchy, just as their forefathers had rebelled against it.

After the Declaration of Independence, the colonies finally considered themselves free of British rule and were ready to draft a new constitution that would replace the old charters. The common law of England was the basis on which they would continue building their own legal system, which would later be adopted by other colonies as they joined the United States of America. The need for English books of law once more grew, and America started printing material such as William Schley's *Digest of the English Statutes* from 1826. This particular work was commissioned by the Georgia legislature, and it included the entire 1225 Magna Carta text.

The American Revolution was a direct rejection of sovereign authority. With the ending of the war in 1783, the thirteen colonies were loosely bound together by the Articles of Confederation and Perpetual Union. However, it became clear that more centralized power was needed to keep the new states bound into a union. In 1787, the Constitution of the United States was born in Philadelphia, and out of it, a new centralized government came to be. The Founding Fathers made sure that this new government could not tyrannize the people of the United States of America but would be strong enough to protect them. The federal Constitution, which was adopted in 1789, was the compromise they came up with to guard the confederation as if it were a single state. The United States Constitution limited the government's power in more than one way. The Magna Carta gave a lesson on why the power of government needed to be constrained for the people to enjoy their liberties. To achieve this, the Constitution separated the government's power into three branches: the legislative, executive, and judicial. Each one of these branches was to act as a restraint to the others' power. The American Constitution also divided responsibilities between the federal government and the states. However, even though they restrict each other's power, it is exactly this division between federal and state sovereignty that has resulted in the conflict that lasts to this day.

As the federal Constitution came to light, the Anti-Federalists protested that there was no document to confirm the freedoms of the people, such as the Magna Carta. The supporters of the federation replied that there was no need for a new Magna Carta, as confirmation of the people's liberties was in the Constitution itself in the form of the first ten amendments known as the American Bill of Rights, ratified in 1791. The First Amendment went much further than the Magna Carta ever did in restraining the government. There was to be no official religion established, no abridgment of the freedom of speech or the press, and no prohibition of peaceable assembly or the petition for a redress of grievances. The Ninth Amendment promised that the enumeration of rights in the bill would neither restrain the people from gaining new rights nor bar them from defending their other rights. Americans had been oppressed by a monarchy and had developed a natural fear of history repeating itself. To prevent their government from acting similar to the English Parliament, they developed a series of constitutional documents that would guarantee their rights and protect them from ever being oppressed again.

It was the Fifth Amendment that was built upon the so well-known Clause 29/39 of the Magna Carta. It promised that no person would be deprived of life, liberty, or property without due process of law. The Sixth Amendment continued by borrowing exact phrases from the Great Charter, such as the "lawful judgment of peers" and "law of the land," while it promised a speedy trial by an impartial jury for those accused of crimes. Criminals gained the right to be informed of the nature of their accusations and the right to defend themselves.

Even though the Magna Carta influenced the Constitution and the Bill of Rights of the United States of America, it lost the central role in the court that it had held during the colonial times. It wasn't forgotten, though, as it was always the document that guaranteed due process to the people of America and, therefore, was held in high regard. Even a Supreme Court justice wrote about the significance of the Charter in 1819, speaking about the lessons mankind learned during the fight to defend their freedoms. The Magna Carta has been cited over a hundred times in Supreme Court sessions, and even today's lawyers cannot resist citing it. For instance, during the famous 1994 sexual harassment case against American President Bill Clinton, the judge ruled against delaying the process during the president's term of office, calling on the guarantees that the Magna Carta gives to the people that even the sovereign is a subject to the law.

The United States Bill of Rights draws directly from the Magna Carta, promising freedoms to the people living on a continent that was unknown to King John or the barons. The Fifth and the Fourteenth Amendment are defined as "due process of law," which guarantees dignity, equality, and freedom to all people living in a republic, yet Americans proved that this concept is flexible.

For a long time, African Americans did not have the same rights and freedoms that were guaranteed by nature to the English settlers on the continent. It was only during the 1930s that the Supreme Court stepped outside the dogmas of earlier ages and revised the Bill of Rights to include citizens of other nationalities under its protections. During the late 1940s, people of African descent finally had the right to go to a public school, which had been reserved only for those of European descent. Segregation was approaching its end when, in 1946, the statues that divided passengers using public transportation were outlawed. However, the Supreme Court took its boldest step in 1954 when it finally admitted the full freedom and equality of African Americans by declaring racially-segregated schools unconstitutional.

The civil liberties in America were at the highest level of threat during the two world wars in the 20th century. During the wars, the restriction of freedom of speech was often tolerated, as was the roundup of radicals or people of "enemy" descent, who were often detained just for being of a certain nationality. For example, during World War II, people of Japanese descent were relocated and incarcerated in internment camps even though they were natural-born American citizens. Their liberties guaranteed by the Bill of Rights were forcefully taken away. Internees often lost their property, as restrictions prohibited them from taking more than they could carry in their arms. Because of the relocation order, many people lost their jobs, and others were simply fired for being of Japanese descent. It was not until 1976 that American President Gerald R. Ford admitted that the internment of the Japanese was wrong and a national mistake. Civil Liberties Act of 1988 granted reparations to the Americans of

Japanese descent who were affected by the actions of US government during the World War II.

Conclusion

The remarkable story of the Magna Carta and its history will never come to an end simply because the document is still alive, well known, and widely celebrated. We, too, are part of its story, which will turn into history for the next generations. Even though the Great Charter changed many times throughout the ages and bears other names in many countries across the world, it still holds the same ideals of liberty that will keep pushing humanity forward.

In this book, the political process of the Magna Carta is fully on display. The reader can enjoy the story—with its remarkable characters—and through the story, the development of one of the world's greatest documents. Even today, humanity is asking the same questions regarding liberties as the barons of John's England, or the Edward Cokes of the Elizabethan and Jacobean eras. Considering the present age, the Magna Carta may seem to be an old institution that is crumbling under the pressure of greedy oligarchs and despots, but its principals, ideas, and guarantees are very much alive. Although we call it by a new name, the Constitution, the Great Charter continues to spread through all spheres of our individual lives. It still protects us from our own government in the same ways it protected the barons from the king's abuse of power. And it is a constant reminder of how everyone is equal in the eyes of the law, with no exemption—even for the rich and powerful.

As a founding cornerstone of the English constitution and the United States Bill of Rights, the Magna Carta is still observed as a bulwark that protects against arbitrary government. Interestingly, it is now celebrated with much more enthusiasm in America than in England. The American Supreme Court continuously cites the Charter, and it is not the only institution to do so. It is often cited in political debates, judicial discussions, and news media, be it in print or digital formats.

The Magna Carta showed its capacity to grow over time. From the barons' uprisings in the 13th century to the American Revolution in the 18th century, the Great Charter proved to be a resilient document. The original document underwent so many changes that what we have today can hardly be called the Magna Carta, but the original principals and ideas are still very much alive in today's statute books. By keeping the tradition of opposing the government's threats to the people's liberties alive, the Magna Carta has its role to play even today. It is still an inspiration to people who seek to overthrow the yolk of tyranny.

Here's another book by Captivating History
that you might be interested in

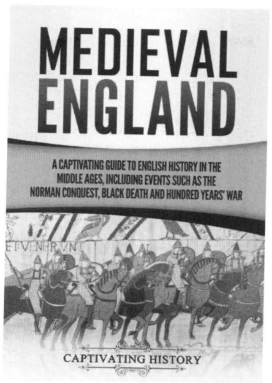

References

Davis, G. R. C. (1999). *Magna Carta*. London: British Library.

Holt, J. C., & Hudson, J. (2015). *Magna Carta*. Cambridge: Cambridge University Press.

Howard, A. E. D. (1968). *The road from Runnymede; Magna Carta and constitutionalism in America*. Charlottesville: University of Virginia Press.

Howard, A. E. D. (1998). *Magna Carta: text and commentary*. Charlottesville: University Press of Virginia.

King, E. (1988). *Medieval England, 1066-1485*. Oxford: Phaidon.

Linebaugh, P. (2008). *The Magna Carta manifesto: liberties and commons for all*. Berkeley: University of California Press.

Morris, M. (2015). *King John: treachery and tyranny in medieval England: the road to Magna Carta*. New York: Pegasus Books.

Printed in Great Britain
by Amazon